This book is due for return on or before the last date shown below.

25 JAN 2000

GETTING TO THE TOP

WOMEN IN MANAGEMENT
WORKBOOK SERIES

GETTING TO THE TOP

GERALDINE BOWN · CATHERINE BRADY

·DOMINO·

KOGAN
PAGE

First published in 1991

Kogan Page Limited
120 Pentonville Road
London N1 9JN

© The Domino Consultancy Ltd, 1991

British Library Cataloguing in Publication Data

A CIP record for this book is available from the British Library.

ISBN 0 7494 0517 1

Typeset by The Castlefield Press Ltd, Wellingborough,
Northants in Palatino 11/12 point.
Printed in England by Clays Ltd. St Ives plc.

Contents

Preface

Welcome to the third in this series of three books under the title The Women in Management Workbook Series.

Getting to the Top considers the steps a woman can take to gain promotion, once she is established in a management post. It looks at the barriers women encounter as they move forward for promotion — both internal and external. There is advice on how to break down those barriers. The book considers leadership skills and the different types of leadership styles. Talks, presentations, meetings and interviews are all good media for demonstrating promotion potential. The book assesses how you can get the most out of these activities. It provides a practical strategy for dealing with the stresses and strains a career in management can bring. Finally it considers ten practical tactics for promotion.

The first book, *Are You Ready to Manage?* was written for women seeking their first management appointment. It assesses skills, qualities and experience and looks at ways of boosting confidence. It also considers the various methods that can be used to find that first appointment, as well as how to settle into a new role.

The second in the series, entitled *The Successful Manager* assesses the different ways a woman manager can make a success of her post. It considers assertiveness and communication at work, how to manage your team and how to manage your time.

The premise of this series is twofold:

- That women in the 1990s are actively seeking management posts of all kinds.
- That women have the ability to fulfil those posts but sometimes lack the self-confidence and the necessary support to move on and up.

These books will help.

They are designed as a practical guide to management . . . not a series on management theory *and* they are written by women. They contain practical advice on how to get where you want to be. There are ideas and tips which you can apply to your own unique situation and which can be adapted for your own purposes. The books are full of case studies — women already in management positions explaining how certain techniques helped them.

The books are to be read proactively — in other words, to get the most out of them, you have to get involved. So read with a pen in your hand. There are charts and check-lists for you to complete — each one taking you further towards your personal management goal!

We wish you every success in your management career.

Geraldine Bown
Managing Director
The Domino Consultancy Limited

ACKNOWLEDGEMENTS

Many people have given their time and expertise in helping us to write this book.

We would like to thank all the women managers who worked with us on this project, providing information for case studies.

We also wish to thank Jan Smith for her cartoons, Zoe Bartells for conducting the research and Ann Baker for editing the series.

The Women in Management Workbook Series

The Domino Consultancy Ltd

A series of three self-assessment workbooks devised specifically for women aiming for a career in management. Each workbook deals with a specific stage in a woman's management career using the same 'action learning' approach which allows for a surprising level of self-awareness. Other titles in the series are:

WORKBOOK 1: ARE YOU READY TO MANAGE?

This, the first book in the series, is for the women considering a first-time career in management. By assessing her skills and experience the reader is able to draw up a personal profile and an action plan for achieving her ultimate career goal.

ISBN 0 7494 0519 8

WORKBOOK 2: THE SUCCESSFUL MANAGER

Aimed at those women who have attained a management position, this book shows how to achieve excellence and professionalism in their work by improving skills in important areas such as communication, team building, time management and assertiveness.

ISBN 0 7494 0518 X

The Domino Consultancy

The Domino Consultancy Ltd is recognised particulary in the UK and abroad for their expertise in the highly specialised and growing area of women's training and development. They are well known for their high quality training materials and their client base includes NatWest, Midland, Barclays and TSB Banks; Shell UK; the AA; Scottish Homes; PowerGen; Harrods; Manchester Airport; Safeway and Marks and Spencer.

Geraldine Bown is the managing director of Domino, the vice president of the European Women's Management Development Network and representative to the European Women's lobby. She is a frequent speaker at conferences here and abroad.

Catherine Brady is a director of Domino and is responsible for all its development and production projects.

While both being successful business women, the authors each have families and, therefore, firsthand experience of balancing the demands of home and work.

Introduction

Moving up the Management Ladder

Compared to ten years ago, women are now well represented in junior management. The situation has been improved by better education, equal opportunities legislation and a change in attitudes within society — away from the woman as 'home-maker' and the man as 'breadwinner'.

Women are more determined than ever to get to the top. The problem seems to be that as they get closer, something stops them — the so-called glass ceiling. This is the intangible barrier that many women encounter as they move up the management scale. This barrier explains why only 4 per cent of management posts at middle and senior level are held by women, and at senior executive level under 2 per cent. This book considers some of the main factors which contribute to this glass ceiling and suggests ways of breaking through.

Even at lower levels of management, women are in the minority. Because of this, they lack role models — other women in a similar position from whom they can learn. The higher up the ladder they climb, the worse this problem becomes.

Some women who have reached the top have done so by adopting an aggressive 'male' style of management, believing they need to work like men in order to compete with men. There may be some truth in this, but for younger women entering the realms of middle and senior management for the first time, it can be confusing.

If a woman has been successful so far in her career by adopting a more cooperative method of working, should she change because she has been promoted? To do so may jeopardise her chances of success, particularly if she was promoted *because* of her cooperative style, not in spite of it.

One chapter of this book is devoted to the whole topic of leadership style. It looks at the various styles of management prevailing within organisations and assesses which is the best style for you.

Any manager wishing to move up, has to adopt a high profile in the company. Promotion does not come to she who waits. It has to be a conscious decision, and it takes energy and determination to succeed. It means being seen to perform well, being visible, and proving that you are ready for the next level.

One of the best tactics for doing this is through speaking — whether this is giving presentations and talks, or just getting your point across at meetings. Speaking in front of an audience is one skill which fills some female managers with trepidation. For their male counterparts, holding the attention of an audience seems almost second nature.

This is partly due to conditioning, as it is acceptable for boys to dominate, assert themselves and say what they think. It is an interesting exercise to sit in a meeting attended by both sexes and observe. Who does most of the talking? Who does most of the interrupting? Whose ideas are adopted in the end?

Women managers have the added disadvantage that because they are usually in the minority, when they do speak, all attention is focused on them to see how well they perform.

Help is at hand! This book looks at the whole area of presentation skills, including ideas for talks, meetings, and job interviews.

This book also discusses pressure and stress. All managers feel pressure — it is almost written into the job description! But at what point does positive pressure become negative stress?

One person's pressure may be another person's stress; therefore it is virtually impossible to generalise on this matter. What is certainly evident from research is that women in management suffer from more sources of stress than do men in management. This is partly due to the relative isolation of being female in a largely male team; partly due to the fact that women still tend to be responsible for the home as well as their own career. The dual responsibility of managing home and work needs a very fine balancing act indeed, and women need a strategy to help them cope.

If you can come to terms with all the factors discussed here — overcome the barriers, define your own style of leadership, increase your visibility and cope with the pressures, you are ready for that key promotion, and this volume includes some tactics which can help.

1
Breaking Down the Barriers

The path to promotion is not without obstacles, for men as well as women. The difference is that for women they seem to be higher and more numerous than for men. What are the barriers faced by women who strive for the top, and what can you, as a female executive, do about them? This chapter considers some of the main ones — both internal and external — and suggests some ways they can be overcome.

To start with, here are some comments from women executives on barriers.

- 'I'm not taken seriously at work, so they wouldn't see me as management potential.'
- 'If I stand up for myself I'm thought to be pushy . . . and they don't like it . . . Some of them feel threatened because I am ambitious.'
- 'I went back to work after a break and found that things had changed so much. I've missed out somewhere along the line. Also, when I went back I'd lost seniority.'
- 'They think I'm working for pin money.'
- 'I'm treated like his daughter . . . we never discuss work . . . sometimes I feel I get put upon.'
- 'We've been told that they don't promote women here.'
- 'Everybody knows . . . to get on here, you have to know the right people.'
- 'You need to be aggressive if you want to be considered for management.'
- 'They think I should be at home looking after the family.'

- ' . . . and the women who do get to the top are not very "feminine".'
- 'If you're a woman you don't get offered management training.'
- 'Things change slowly . . .'.
- 'Women are better at personnel than at management.'
- 'I think you've either got it or you haven't.'

These comments women made about themselves and their organisations highlight some of the main problems. Very few of these statements could have been made by or about men. This illustrates the need for women's problems at work to be treated as a separate issue. Firstly, let us consider the barriers to career development caused by self-imposed limitations.

INTERNAL BARRIERS

Although it is not the whole truth, it is often said that women are their own worst enemy. The way you think about yourself can stop you from achieving what you want. This is certainly true for women whose self-defeating attitudes prevent them from achieving the top jobs at work. Just because you may have thought about yourself in a certain way in the past, does not mean that you have to continue to do so in the future. Experience shows that by becoming aware of what you do and your underlying motives, you can overcome some of the problems — and move forward.

What are these barriers or mental blocks that some women impose on themselves? Twelve statements cover the main internal barriers women build for themselves.

Twelve internal barriers

1. 'I couldn't possibly . . .'

How many times do you find yourself turning down opportunities because you say to yourself: 'I'd love that job, but I couldn't possibly . . .' or 'I'd really like to train for that career, but I couldn't possibly . . .'

It is the 'buts' of this world which prevent people from succeeding. They impose limits on their capabilities and restrict potential. Women in particular, tend to emphasise what they cannot do and omit what they can do.

To some extent, this habit is understandable when you consider that from an early age women are taught to think that they are good at some things, and not very good at others. Consequently, women do not put themselves forward when opportunities arise. In fact, there is no limit to what you can achieve if you put your mind to it and accept yourself as an individual.

2. *'I don't really want to be an authority figure.'*

Whatever the circumstances or objectives, whatever the material or budget, as a manager, you have to take control. This involves solving problems and making decisions; taking responsibility and being accountable to someone else. To run anything well you have to take charge, and there are some women who hold back from this.

Women often take a secondary role as carers, supporters and subordinates, and therefore do not find it easy to see themselves in positions of authority. They feel uncomfortable in positions of power, and do not put themselves forward when the opportunities are up for grabs, or they do a manager's job half-heartedly because they do not like being the boss.

Being a leader does not have to mean adopting an autocratic style of management. New, participative styles of management are often more suited to a woman's natural style of cooperation, cohesion and joint decision-making. You will have a chance to look at this in more detail later.

3. *'I don't want to be seen as "pushy".'*

Women who make it to positions of power are often described as 'pushy', by some men — and women. This is often because some of the qualities which are seen as desirable in a man are seen as unacceptable in a woman. Someone who speaks up for herself, makes herself known, and takes an active role at work is susceptible to accusations of 'unfeminine' or 'feminist' behaviour.

It is true to say that there are some women who have adopted an aggressive style of management, because they see this as the only way to succeed. However, it is possible for a woman manager to do her job effectively in an assertive way — by standing up for herself, without putting other people down.

4. 'I want to be liked.'

Some women have an excessive need to be liked. They find it difficult to break free from early conditioning which places great emphasis on suppressing personal inclinations in order to respond to other people's needs. This can be destructive if ambitions become subordinated to the need for approval. A manager's wanting to be liked by everyone at all times results in failure to make unpopular decisions, failure to issue instructions, refusal of unreasonable requests, and so on.

Assess your current role and ask yourself: 'Am I here to perform or to please?' and 'Am I more effective when pleasing myself or pleasing others?' It is nice to care what others think — but not to the extent that it stifles your effectiveness now and ambition for the future.

5. 'I want to get this right first.'

Many women have a 'perfection block'. They feel they have to do one job perfectly before they can think of seeking the next rung up the ladder. Ambitious men think differently. In mapping out a career path, men work at their present job, while keeping an eye on what they need to do for the next one. In contrast, women become obsessed with perfect standards and are overtaken when it comes to promotion.

6. *'I'm seen as a daughter/mother/wife.'*

Many women are seen in a family role at work and may find that it cramps their ability to do a good job. As a result of their traditional roles as 'carers', women are often called upon to solve problems and lend a sympathetic ear when a different type of approach may be needed at work.

7. *'But I'm only a . . . '*

. . . housewife, a junior manager, a supervisor, a woman. This way of thinking reflects a lack of self-confidence to do anything other than what you have always done. It encourages other people to see you in a limited role, and, by speaking about yourself in this way, you are refusing to recognise the many skills that these other roles have given you.

Believing that gender or present occupation prevents people from doing certain things is opting for security and denial of the opportunities that a few risks might bring.

8. *'I'm not the type . . . '*

Some people are born with a head start in the management stakes because they seem to have the qualities or charisma that others lack. There is even a belief in some quarters that managers are born to lead. If there is such a 'type' and you do not see yourself fitting into it, then training and self-development will make little difference. People say, 'I'm not the type', when refusing training or promotion, when explaining why they were not selected for the job, or when making excuses for poor job performance. The saying 'I'm not the type' shifts responsibility away from them and guarantees that they never move very far in their chosen career.

9. *'I'll see what the company has in mind for me.'*

Many women miss promotion because they wait for the organisation to take notice of them. They think that for being good at their job, conscientious, and loyal, they will be rewarded. This way of thinking is unproductive because it does not necessarily get results. Opportunities do not usually fall into your lap — you have to go out and find them. Also it means being dependent upon the organisation for your development needs. Thinking like this means handing control of your life to others; maybe sacrificing your career progress to theirs.

10. *'Things change slowly.'*

Some women believe that they will not get very far in the promotion stakes because *any* progress to improve a woman's prospects is slow. They say things such as:

- 'We're stuck because of old values.'
- 'In this place it's not what you know; it's who you know.'
- 'They don't promote women here.'
- 'Perhaps the next generation will find it easier.'

For some women at least, there is some truth in all of these statements, but beliefs such as these will not get you anywhere. If you want changes for the better, whether at home or at work, you have to take responsibility for yourself and make things happen. If the company will not change, then change company!

11. *'I'm not very ambitious.'*

Some people associate ambition with greed, selfishness, and being a workaholic. It is not surprising that this notion exists, as many 'high-flyers' concentrate on work to the exclusion of everything else in their lives. Telling yourself that you are not ambitious limits your potential. It guarantees that you will stay where you are, as other people will assume that you are content with the work and responsibilities that you have at present. Saying such things at work reinforces the negative impression that many managers and other staff already hold of women.

12. 'I'm frightened of power/success.'

You may have ambivalent feelings towards promotion because you fear the power and success associated with it, even though you would like the responsibility, interest and benefits of the job. You may harbour such feelings for a number of reasons:

- You fear not being liked.
- You do not want to make decisions.
- You fear you may not be able to maintain the standard expected of you.
- You fear you may 'let down' those who appointed you.
- You do not know how to handle certain people.
- You cannot see yourself coping with the demands of the job.

These are just a few of the reasons why women jeopardise their own success through fear of the consequences that promotion may bring.

Do any of these 12 barriers apply to you?

Tick the barriers which apply to you and then read the feedback for the ones you have ticked. If none apply, move straight on to the discussion of external barriers.

My barriers to success

I couldn't possibly . . .	☐
I don't really like being an authority figure.	☐
I don't want to be seen as 'pushy'.	☐
I want to be liked.	☐
I want to get this right first.	☐
I'm seen as a daughter/mother/wife.	☐
But I'm only a . . .	☐
I'm not the type.	☐
I'll see what the company has in mind for me.	☐
Things change slowly.	☐
I'm not very ambitious.	☐
I'm frightened of power/success.	☐

How can you overcome these internal barriers to success?

Overcoming my barriers to success

1. 'I couldn't possibly . . .'

If you want to be in control of your life, you have to learn to take a few risks and make some decisions for yourself. This means that you have to stop using negatives such as 'can't'. Try telling yourself that you *can*, and see what changes this can bring about.

2. 'I don't really want to be an authority figure.'

If you want to move into — or up to — senior management, you need to welcome authority, and learn how to use it well. It does not mean that you have to browbeat others in order to do the job. There are ways of handling authority which can make the job easier and more pleasant for all concerned.

3. 'I don't want to be seen as "pushy".'

You do not have to be. Many women are not happy imitating a 'male style'. It does not suit their nature — or the nature of the job — to get things done in this way. What is the alternative? Be yourself — and use your 'female' strengths. This way, you will feel better in the role, and you will be more effective because of this.

4. 'I want to be liked.'

This need to be liked by everyone is unrealistic and discourages you from getting the job you really want. How realistic is it to think in this way? Do you like everybody that you come into contact with during the course of your work? Just because somebody does not like you, do not assume that you are not doing a good job. If you want to be liked by everyone, it will impair your ability to do a manager's job well.

5. 'I want to get this right first.'

In concentrating on perfecting your present skills, you are neglecting the skills that you need for your next job. 'Perfection' is not usually high on the list in a job specification. As the saying goes, not everything worth doing is worth doing well!

6. 'I'm seen as a daughter/mother/wife.'

Do not encourage people, particularly men, to treat you in this way. If people expect you to solve their problems, 'kiss where it hurts', and 'make everything better', it will make demands upon your efforts, your energy and your time. As a manager, you may lose credibility. Not that your caring side should never be seen. Just make sure that it does not affect your ability to do a good job.

7. 'But I'm only a . . .'

To get the promotion you want — and deserve — you have to be able to sell yourself, and this means eliminating words such as 'only' and 'just' from your everyday speech. Recognise your strengths and promote them.

8. 'I'm not the type.'

Put this out of your mind. The first thing to grasp about management — or leadership — is that nobody, not even a prime minister, is born knowing how to do it. There is no such thing as 'the management type'. Some people do start off with more advantages than others, in terms of personal characteristics; but for the rest, there is no substitute for training and experience.

9. 'I'll see what the company has in mind for me.'

If you want to be responsible for others, you have to start by assuming responsibility for yourself. Gone are the days when you looked to the organisation to provide your guidance and training needs. Self-development is the emphasis of the future.

10. *'Things change slowly.'*

Despite all the laws to improve career prospects for women, discrimination is still rife for many women at work. Many organisations offer little incentive to women to move into management, particularly if there is a large pool of male talent waiting to be tapped. Your best course of action will depend upon your circumstances, your goals and your resources. You might like to consider doing one of the following:

- find out what management training is available within your organisation and make the necessary moves to put yourself forward;
- develop the skills and qualities that the company requires of senior managers;
- make your ambitions known and get yourself noticed.

If your present job has no future, and you feel that you are not going to get anywhere with your organisation, then you may need to look elsewhere. Many companies are actively encouraging more women to apply for management positions because of the skills and qualities that women offer. Do not wait for things to change — make things happen for yourself!

11. *'I'm not very ambitious.'*

Being ambitious does not mean you have to aim for the top of the tree, because much will depend upon your personal values and circumstances. Choose your goal, and channel your energies into getting that. Ambition does not mean that you have to sacrifice all other values, interests, and people in your life. Many men and women have learned, to their cost, the consequences of a life which is exclusively centred on work and work-related issues. Being ambitious means that you want to make the most of your talents, your potential and your life. Find a goal to aim towards and make a move towards it now!

12. *'I'm frightened of power/success.'*

Learn to assess 'success' realistically in terms of the benefits that it can bring to your life. If you want the power to influence and change things, then seize all opportunities that you get to sit in the 'hot seat'.

All these beliefs that women have about themselves arise from a lack of self-confidence. Men also have inhibitions which get in the way of career advancement, but they do not emphasise them in the way that women often do. Now that you have looked at personal perceptions which can restrict opportunities, consider some of the barriers which are imposed by organisations.

EXTERNAL BARRIERS

'Why not train more women for management?' is a question often put to those in organisations who are interested in finding the right people for key management positions. There is no end to the variety of responses which are given in answer to this. Here are some of them:

1. 'We don't need to — there are plenty of able men.'

2. 'It's not cost-effective to train women for upper management.'

3. 'Why should we change what is working well?'

4. 'Our women won't attend training courses.'

5. 'We've had women in higher management, and it doesn't always work.'

6. 'Women don't have the right qualifications.'

7. 'Women are just not interested in middle- and senior-management positions.'

Consider each one of these arguments more closely.

Seven external barriers

1. *'We don't need to — there are plenty of able men.'*

Are there no able women? At present, there is a national shortage of highly skilled staff right across the jobs spectrum, including management. Provision for training in this country is woefully inadequate, and organisations are constantly looking for people with the right combination of qualities and skills.

Research shows that women have skills which could complement those of men, and help to create a stronger, more balanced senior management team. With a large pool of skills available among the female workforce, it does not make sense to waste these skills.

2. *'It's not cost-effective to train women for upper management.'*

The old argument is that it is pointless to train women because they leave when they have a family. The facts contradict this. Between the ages of 20 and 59, most women are in continuous employment of some kind. The career break for those who leave to have children is from three to seven years, and even shorter for those in a professional career. Moreover, the number of younger career women choosing not to have children is increasing.

Those organisations which have career break schemes have found that professional skills, once taught, are never forgotten. Those women who are treated well by their companies tend to repay them with many years of loyal service. Finally, it is true to say that highly trained men do not necessarily repay the investment made in their training by staying with the company. Those who are ambitious will move on when they get the opportunity.

3. *'Why should we change what is working well?'*

Is it really working well? Successful organisations are those which are flexible and can adapt to change. What works well now may not work quite so well in the future. With a fluctuating economy and a workforce whose expectations of work and employment have changed dramatically over the last few years, organisations are having to look at new patterns of working. The introduction of more women at middle- and senior-management level may be just the opportunity that an organisation needs to cope with more radical changes resulting from the Single European Market.

4. *'Our women won't attend training courses.'*

If this is the case, does anybody bother to find out why? There are many reasons why women do not always take advantage of the management training available.

- Management training may not be available to everybody. This can be difficult to find out about. You may need to hear about it through the grapevine.
- Women may not be asked if they wish to attend. They are less likely than men to be identified for development, and they often receive less encouragement to manage their careers.
- Women may not have identified their own training needs. Since women often do not plan their careers like men, they do not always look at the training they will need for the next step on the ladder.
- Women may not want to be in a minority of one or two in an otherwise all-male training programme.
- The timing of the course might make it difficult for women to attend. How many women can attend a five-day residential course far from home, with the needs of young children to consider?
- Women may see the course as irrelevant to their needs. When everything is seen from a male perspective and assumptions are made that managers are male, women feel excluded.

5. *'We've had women in higher management, and it doesn't always work.'*

Perhaps not, but companies need to look at the problems

that women managers have, in order to improve things. Some women in senior positions feel isolated, and unsure of how to behave. They do not have role models to draw upon in adopting a management style. Consequently, they often try to imitate male managers, or they adopt a passive role. Either way, they are not effective managers. Also, their job may become more difficult because the men and women they work with are not used to seeing women in top management and may feel threatened. This may create pressures which are difficult to cope with.

As the number of women in management roles increases, women will feel more confident in their ability to do the job by being themselves. This, in turn, will clear the path for other women. The response made here is not a sufficient reason to bar all women from showing how well they can succeed in a high-level management job.

6. *'Women don't have the right qualifications.'*

Some women feel their path is blocked because they do not have formal business qualifications. Many organisations, however, look for job applicants with a combination of personal qualities and experience — people with talent. This is seen in general terms as 'bright', 'ambitious', or 'right personality', rather than in terms of educational qualifications. It is up to women to recognise and sell the qualities and skills that they have.

7. *'Women are just not interested in middle- and senior-management posts.'*

The facts do not support this. Women are better educated than they used to be. The majority accept that they will spend a good percentage of their lives in paid employment. More and more women are looking for a career which provides stimulation, rewards and job satisfaction.

Moreover, women are beginning to recognise that they are ideally suited to management because of their breadth of skills and experience and wider perspective. Yes, they will make their career a top priority — but not to the exclusion of everything else. Their wider interests mean they have much more to offer an organisation than is offered by the 12 hours a day, 'company man' approach.

You may have noted that some of these arguments had been used to dissuade or discourage you from considering a particular management post in the past. Were you satisfied with the response you then made? You may find that you have to counter arguments such as these when requesting training or development, even at interview. Make sure you know how to respond to scepticism about an expanding role for women in management. Not everybody is going to be convinced by what you say. It is not in the interests of some people to concede that you may be right. If they did accept your arguments, they might be forced to show their commitment by actually doing something, such as finding out what is going on in their own organisation, and then taking measures to combat any discrimination which exists.

More women in management inevitably means fewer men. This may be justified in terms of numbers, but an appeal for 'fairness' has never won many votes.

However, some senior managers may ponder what you have said. Maybe those with the power to change things will recognise what is going on and realise that it is in their interests too, to strengthen the management sector of the organisation.

The following case studies show how two senior women managers overcame their external barriers.

Case studies

Finance manager in a large manufacturing company

'When I was in a previous post, I qualified with the accountancy body, CIMA. The men who travelled the same route as myself were then promoted to junior management positions. So I thought, what's happening here? Initially, I approached my manager, as I felt that as I was qualified I should be given the same opportunities. The approach was successful. My career progression has been fairly rapid since, and this job is a senior management post.

You have to put yourself forward.'

Carol Bode, Training Manager, Automobile Association Insurance Services, Head Office, Basingstoke

'I have doubted my own capabilities on occasions throughout my management career, but experience has taught me to always try and put things in context. My previous job was in retailing where I enjoyed rapid promotion in the early years. However, I hit barriers when I reached a middle-management post and had moved into the area of the old boy network. Being a female in a traditionally male environment, it was made clear that I would have to bide my time before I moved into senior management. I wasn't prepared to sit and wait, so I looked for another opportunity to develop my career. This came in the offer of a senior-management post in a different organisation, so I moved. Looking back, I don't think I would have overcome that barrier had I stayed.

Remember:

She who gets hired
is not necessarily the one
who can do that job best,
but the one who knows
the most about
how to get hired.

2
Leadership Skills

The role of leader within a group is a highly complex phenomenon, subject to group consensus, group dynamics and many other factors. This chapter does not cover the theoretical aspects of leadership, but concentrates instead on some of the general rules and pitfalls of leadership which will be of practical use to you. It considers your own leadership potential and style.

HAVE I GOT WHAT IT TAKES TO BE A LEADER?

You want to be in charge, but have you got what it takes?

Read through the questions on pages 34 and 35 and tick the columns which apply to you.

Now that you have assessed your leadership potential, look at each of these characteristics in turn, to see how they are relevant to the role of leader.

1. 'Can I motivate people?'

Management entails getting the job done as quickly and as efficiently as possible by using all available resources. Your most valuable resource is your staff, and therefore it makes sense to ensure that they are well motivated to work.

If you manage a group of subordinates, your responsibility is to provide encouragement in order to get the best out of them. Effective teamwork will ultimately lead to success. Some people have a natural enthusiasm and talent for motivating others; some have a high degree of self-motivation but need to learn specific skills for helping others to perform well at work. Thus, training and self-development may be the answer.

2. 'Could I criticise my staff if necessary?'

Managers have a duty to improve and maintain the performance of their staff, and this involves criticising their work from time to time. Women often shy away from this task because they fear unpleasant repercussions and the risk that they may not be liked. Criticism is never pleasant, but it does not have to be destructive. It is often given in such a way that the self-esteem of the person being criticised is damaged and the criticism goes unheeded. Criticism can lead to a break-down in relationships if it is approached in a totally negative and unhelpful way.

It does not have to be like this. The manager who approaches the task with tact and sensitivity will take steps to ensure that:

- the time and place are chosen carefully;
- it is specific aspects of the poor performance which are criticised — and not the person;
- standards for improvement are established and agreed;
- there is an opportunity for members of staff to state any problems that may be adversely affecting their work.

3. 'Am I willing to put the needs of the organisation before the needs of the employees?'

Your ultimate responsibility is to get the job done. This means considering the needs of the employees and those of the organisation. You have to learn to balance both sets of needs in order to cope with any conflict that might arise. However, there may be occasions when you are in the position of having to do things such as disciplining or even firing an employee. This is a responsibility you must be prepared to accept.

Have I got what it takes to be leader?

	yes sometimes	yes always	don't know	no seldom	no never
1. Can I motivate people?					
2. Could I criticise my staff if necessary?					
3. Am I willing to put the needs of the organisation before the needs of the employees?					
4. Do I want power?					
5. Would I fall apart if criticised?					
6. Do I have high levels of energy?					
7. Am I good at making quick decisions?					
8. Will I have problems in delegating some tasks?					
9. Am I prepared to take risks?					

	sometimes	always	don't know	seldom	never
10. Am I friendly and approachable?					
11. Can I cope with failure and setbacks?					
12. Can I challenge instructions from higher management?					
13. Am I prepared to be accountable for mistakes made by my staff?					
14. Can I go away and do things without constantly checking back?					
15. Can I cope with the pressure?					
16. Will it matter to me if my staff dislike me?					
17. Will it matter to me if colleagues disagree with my way of working?					
18. Can I handle being misquoted or misunderstood?					
19. Is work a priority for me at present?					
20. Have I got the determination to succeed against all the odds?					

4. *'Do I want power?'*

All leaders have power, to a lesser or greater extent. Organisations cannot function without authority, and authority brings power.

Power is a concept that frightens some women because they associate it with its misuse or even abuse. But power does not have to be a negative concept. If you want the capacity to influence people and events and create changes in line with your ideas and values, then you must welcome and actively seek power. Learn to feel comfortable with it and to use it well.

5. *'Would I fall apart if criticised?'*

You have to learn to accept criticism — not only of your own performance, but of that of your staff, too. Try not to let criticism affect your self-worth. Some people make it appear to be a personal attack. If you find yourself on the receiving end of destructive criticism, try to establish what exactly was wrong and how it can be put right.

Women are often said to be poor at receiving criticism. For this reason, managers avoid giving them feedback on their performance because they fear a poor reaction. In order to improve your performance and be seen as somebody who is keen to succeed, you need to ask for and welcome feedback.

6. *'Do I have high levels of energy?'*

The demands of management are such that you need to have high levels of energy. Take steps to ensure that the negative effects of any job stresses are diminished. Look at your role in a positive way, viewing problems as challenges that require creative solutions. It helps to make sure that you are fit and healthy, and to spend time on the things and with the people that are important to you — in order to achieve a happy balance between home and work.

7. *'Am I good at making quick decisions?'*

When dealing with a crisis or the unexpected at work, you have to be able to make quick decisions, often without all the necessary information to hand. You must learn to trust your own judgement and to take risks. Many women are skilled at 'crisis management', having learned to do many things at once and to make quick decisions. When unexpected problems arise, it is the woman who defines priorities, decides on a course of action, follows it through, evaluates its success, and restores harmony when it has passed. This ability, like most others, is a transferable skill that you should promote.

8. *'Will I have problems in delegating some tasks?'*

Women often have trouble in delegating because they hold on tightly to their areas of expertise, and find it difficult to ask others to do things for them. You have to delegate because you will not have time to do all your assigned tasks yourself. Moreover, delegating is a method of developing and using the skills of your staff, and showing that you have confidence in their abilities. It is an essential element of motivating your team.

9. *'Am I prepared to take risks?'*

Any decision-making process involves an element of risk, and the higher up the management ladder you climb, the more you have to take risks. Much depends upon your attitude towards your role. If you enjoy making decisions, you will welcome the risks as challenges to your skill and creativity. Remember — growth is slower, personal or otherwise, without some element of risk.

10. *'Am I friendly and approachable?'*

Good management thrives on the ability to get on with people. The more approachable you are, the more likely it is that relationships with your staff will be good and productive. You will get to hear of problems before they become crises. You will be kept informed of things that you should know. It will be easier for you to instruct and motivate staff.

It is not suggested that you should smile and be friendly in circumstances that do not warrant this type of approach. You need not have an 'open door' policy — a friendly, not-too-distant approach which shows that you are aware of other people's abilities, needs and problems, will create the best working atmosphere for everyone.

11. *'Can I cope with failure and setbacks?'*

Everyone suffers from failure and setbacks at some point in life — it helps to remember that! What matters most is how you cope. Failing in a task does not mean that you have failed as a person. Thinking this is destructive, and causes you to lose confidence in yourself. Get into the habit of evaluating what went wrong and what went right, after the event. This way you can try to avoid making the same mistakes again. Learn to recognise your strengths and weaknesses, and accept that perfection may be an unrealistic goal.

12. *'Can I challenge instructions from higher management?'*

If you are issued with instructions which you think are unsatisfactory or unworkable, you may need to challenge them. This does not mean that you have to adopt an aggressive approach — in fact, this style of operating is less likely to bring about a negotiated settlement. A direct but tactful approach will be respected and remembered.

13. *'Am I prepared to be accountable for mistakes made by my staff?'*

You cannot disclaim responsibility for errors made by your staff on the grounds that it was not your error. As a manager, you have to be accountable for what goes wrong, and to take the necessary steps to ensure that it does not happen again. You will get the blame occasionally, but remember you will also get the credit when things go well.

14. *'Can I go away and do things without constantly checking back?'*

Once you have been given a task or a responsibility you will be expected to get on with it. Learn to trust your own judgement, and to be less reliant on others. Show that you can get things done by applying your own special skills to problems that may defeat others.

15. *'Can I cope with the pressure?'*

You can cope with it more effectively if you can channel it into positive action. Pressure does not have to be a negative force — that is, 'stress'. A certain amount of pressure is necessary to motivate, and it can act as a great stimulus to creativity. Learn to recognise how much pressure you can stand before it begins to have a negative effect. It is impossible to avoid it completely, but you can diminish its more harmful effects if you take some precautions.

16. *'Will it matter to me if my staff dislike me?'*

You have a duty to perform, not an obligation to please your staff. If you defer carrying out your responsibilities because you are worried about 'not being liked', you will not be fulfilling your job requirements. From time to time, all managers have to make unpopular decisions, issue instructions and make changes at work. However, you are usually judged by others on the basis of all your actions, not just one or two. Wanting to be liked all the time will impair your effectiveness as a manager, and your credibility as a leader.

17. *'Will it matter to me if colleagues disagree with my ways of working?'*

You cannot please all of the people all of the time. This holds true for your subordinates and other managers alike. You may evoke disapproval among your colleagues, particularly if your 'style' seems to be at odds with what they have come to expect. It is for you to find and establish a style that suits both you and your team.

18. 'Can I handle being misquoted or misunderstood?'

Even if you pride yourself on your system of 'open communication' at work, you may still find that you are misquoted or misunderstood by accident or design. The best tactic is to try to establish what has been said, and to identify the motives involved. This sort of situation often arises from insecurity when employees suspect that management is withholding information or working against them. It is less likely to happen if you have clear and direct lines of communication which provide a forum where contentious issues can be discussed.

19. 'Is work a priority for me at present?'

If you are aspiring to advance within management, work must be one of your top priorities. Your priorities are determined by your use of time, and if you want to make a successful career in management, you have to be prepared to spend time and energy in achieving this success. Work has to be a priority — but not the only one. More and more managers are realising that to be effective, you do not have to work a 60-hour week. You can give time and commitment to other areas of your life and still be a good manager and leader. Most people find fulfilment in a life which allows time for people and interests unconnected with work, and more and more organisations are realising that fact.

20. 'Have I got the determination to succeed against all the odds?'

You will need all the determination you can muster to overcome the barriers that women may face when they try to establish a career in higher management. Do not give up; confidence and perseverance are usually rewarded!

Go back to the questionnaire you completed on leadership and consider carefully the areas where you have particular difficulties. Identify ways in which you can improve your capacity for leadership.

Improving my leadership potential

I am going to:

LEADERSHIP STYLE

Manager 1 sits in the office with the door closed; if subordinates want to discuss an issue, they knock and wait until invited to enter. This manager makes all decisions and tells them what has been decided — and does not believe in consultation.

Manager 2 works alongside the team. This manager is in charge, responsible and accountable — but knows that the best results are achieved through joint efforts.

These are two examples of leadership style — how you get things done at work. As a manager, you need to find out how you are going to perform most effectively. Style is important for the following reasons:

■ It influences how you are seen by your employers.
■ It affects the way you see yourself.
■ It determines your relationship with your staff.

If the best of me can make more of you, then the best of you will reflect on me.

But what is meant by 'leadership style'? There are three main traditional leadership styles, which will be assessed in a moment. Will you take up one of these styles, or adopt a new approach of your own?

As one woman manager found out, the secret is — do not be too quick to change.

Case study

Anne Jessopp, Divisional Personnel Manager, Radio Rentals, Central Division

I think you have to be mindful of the organisation you're in, but carry on with your own style as far as possible. I'm lucky that my participative style suits the organisation. Some women think that when they're promoted, they should adopt a different style. In fact, this wouldn't fit in with the organisation and can be extremely stressful for the individual.

If you've been promoted through a company it's essential to remember that you've been promoted for who you are and you should continue with that successful formula. My personal style is to involve my staff and get them to suggest ideas and make it a two-way thing. One of the transitions in managing which can be difficult to get used to is being able to recognise that the success of your staff is your success.

Traditional leadership styles

Traditional leadership styles can be classified as:

1. autocratic
2. laissez-faire
3. participative.

Each has its own characteristics and benefits to you as the leader. They also have both positive and negative effects on staff you manage.

Autocratic

This is the traditional model of leadership, still widely used, particularly in organisations which have a strongly hierarchical structure.

Characteristics

- Managers who adopt this style of managing rely on their power and position to get things done.
- They like people to acknowledge their status and power.
- Once they have made a decision, they rarely change their minds.
- They see flexibility as a weakness.
- They decide what action to take and issue instructions, often accompanied by threats or punishments.
- They rarely give consideration to what their staff will feel about a particular decision, and give no opportunity for their staff to participate.
- They respect loyalty and will not tolerate dissent.
- They communicate mostly in writing.
- They discourage creative thinking as it is seen as a challenge to authority.
- They like to keep information to themselves.
- They rarely delegate.
- They like workers who conform to their rigid standards.
- Autocratic leaders focus on the task, rather than individual involvement or motivation.
- They prefer to deal with people individually rather than to deal with the uncertainty of group behaviour, so they tend not to hold meetings.

Pay-offs

- Decisions are reached more quickly when they are made by one person.
- The leader takes personal credit when things go well.
- Their authoritarian position may enhance their status and authority in other people's eyes. People may admire their 'strength' and 'clarity of vision'.

Positive effects

- When a leader is in charge of people who are unable or unwilling to share responsibility, this style of leadership may work well.
- People who do routine, repetitive jobs may not be looking for challenge or involvement.
- There are some personality types who do not respond well to change and flexibility, and prefer the type of authoritarian rule which characterises this management style.
- In circumstances such as a crisis, this directive style may work best because people need to know that somebody is in charge who can make quick decisions, when necessary.
- People feel secure with rules and authority. It is predictable and they 'know where they stand'.

Negative effects

- Staff respond through fear but are usually dissatisfied with this managerial behaviour, leading to resentment, frustration and stifling of initiative.
- Lack of involvement in decisions which affect their working lives can also reduce the commitment of employees, who feel that they have no autonomy or control.
- There is often poor morale and high staff turnover.
- People often try to sabotage the actions of this type of leader by agreeing in principle to what is decided, but refusing to conform in practice.
- Relations among workers can be divisive as they compete for favour and rewards.
- Poor productivity levels can result.
- Low creativity and ultimate stagnation result within the organisation.

Laissez-faire

These managers are the most casual of all, and it is tempting to drift into this style of leadership if you have accepted the role of manager reluctantly, unexpectedly or with uncertainty about your ability to do the job.

Characteristics

- The laissez-faire type of leader issues general rules and guidelines to the group, and then tries not to get involved unless requested to do so.
- There is no discipline imposed on the group. Members choose with whom they will work, and tasks are usually decided by group decision.
- The group defines the problems, seeks alternative solutions and makes all decisions.
- Mistakes are overlooked.

Pay-offs

- The leader does not have to lead.
- The leader does not have to issue instructions.
- The leader does not have to make decisions.
- The leader does not have to face conflict.
- The leader does not have to take risks.
- The leader does not feel the need to accept responsibility.
- The leader may retain popularity — for a while.
- The leader can behave like one of the team, while benefiting from a leader's status and salary.

Positive effects

- People have a certain independence and do not have to work closely with other members of the team. With highly motivated people, this approach may sometimes work. For example, a research group in which scientists, technicians and engineers are granted the

freedom to solve problems as they see fit might work well under this style of leadership.
- People are not directly accountable for their mistakes or shortcomings.

Negative effects

- This style of leadership can frustrate members of a team who feel that their leader is weak and ineffectual because she is not fulfilling their expectations of how a leader should behave.
- Staff may resent the amount of responsibility which they are carrying without the accompanying status or salary.
- Relations between leader and staff are probably strained, and there is a possibility of chaos as people drift away in different directions.

Participative

Characteristics

- A participative leader focuses on building a team and using the expertise of each member of that team.
- Leaders meet frequently with the team to create a strong team spirit. They understand the power of groups and the benefit of communicating in a group setting.
- There is much face-to-face communication.
- There are many meetings.
- Leaders involve the team in decision-making by proposing a plan, inviting comments and making possible amendments. They do not give up responsibility or control, as they always make the final decision themselves.
- Managers need to have good interpersonal and communication skills, and have to share the sort of information that autocratic leaders would keep to themselves.

Pay-offs

- Teamwork gets good results.
- Working relationships are good.
- Tasks and responsibilities are shared.

Positive effects

- This style offers a good working relationship between team and leader. The team is involved but does not carry the responsibility for making the decision.
- When people are involved in decision-making that influences their work, they are usually more committed to the outcome of these decisioins. They have a feeling of responsibility.

Negative effects

- Some people may not want this amount of involvement.
- As information is shared between leader and team, there has to be a high degree of trust between them. Problems arise for both if this trust is breached.
- Team members must be able to feel that their ideas are taken notice of. There may be resentment if their suggestions are not incorporated into the final solution.
- Consultation is time-consuming.
- Success will be jeopardised if this way of working is imposed upon the members of a team.

You may not have been familiar with the names given to these ways of working, but you probably recognised managers you have known from the descriptions of each one. You may even have identified your *own* style.

Now it is time to find out about you. What is *your* leadership style?

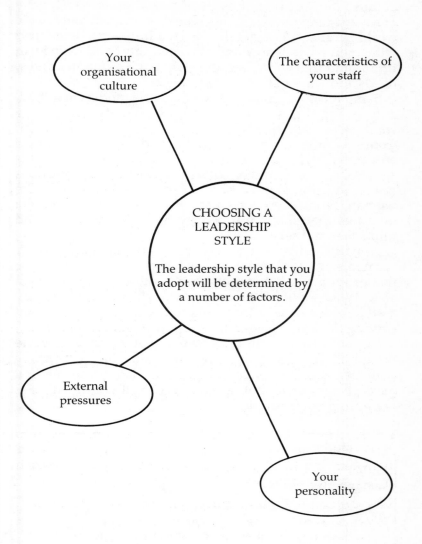

Leadership style is a terrible dilemma for many women because they are often unsure of how they should behave in a management role. It may seem like an alien and hostile world because it is a largely male environment, developed with men's needs in mind. Women are handicapped in fitting into this world because they have different values, needs and ways of looking at things.

Being the only woman, having no role models to follow, and feeling that she has to adopt a stereotyped role are some of the situations that a woman may find herself in. Consequently, many women have chosen to adopt an autocratic style of leadership in order to fit in. This aggressive, competitive, confrontational style often does not go down well with others. It can cause problems for the woman, too, if it goes against her natural tendencies. She may feel that she is trapped by her role, restricted and unlike her real self.

A participative style may be more suited to many women's natural way of working, but it may be inappropriate to the organisation's culture or the needs of staff. What should the woman do? If she does not identify a style of leadership that suits her, she may find herself drifting towards a laissez-faire role with all its problems.

Do not despair. It does seem that more and more organisations are recognising the value of participative management. Do not be too quick to change your natural management style, but do not forget that you can always learn from other people.

Case study

Catherine Carruthers, Project Manager, Business in the Community

> My situation at the moment means I'm working with a person who is on secondment from another company. I'm learning a lot about how that company operates and how I operate. I see it as an opportunity for me to learn, improve, change and grow while remaining true to my own management style. If you abandon your own style and force yourself to fit in you will become uncomfortable and won't manage effectively.

A new approach

Major changes have taken place in society in the last few years which have greatly altered the world of work. The introduction of new technology, economic instability, and intense global competition mean that organisations have to cope with constant changes in order to survive. Moreover, people have changed too. A report entitled *Management of the Future*, (Barham, K, Fraser, J and Heath, L, 1988, for the Foundation for Management Education/Ashridge Management College) states:

> A better educated and more sophisticated workforce, incorporating a high proportion of so-called 'knowledge workers', increasingly wishes to be involved in, or be consulted about, decisions which affect their working lives, and has come to view job satisfaction as a right. It is also a workforce which has come to be impatient with autocratic management styles, and with formality and status-consciousness . . . The workforce is likely to contain a wide variety of values and lifestyles. These changes in expectations reinforce the importance of measures to involve and motivate employees.

People now expect more satisfaction and fulfilment in their working lives. Organisations have to respond to this if they want to attract and keep their highly skilled workforce. As a result, many organisations are now reassessing their attitudes towards what they expect of their managers. To give just one example, many companies are finding that career mobility can no longer be demanded as part and parcel of the job, when young managers with working partners are reluctant to move every few years.

The old style of management with its emphasis on tough-mindedness and competition is under attack. People are rejecting the old limiting patterns of management, and are seeking a lifestyle that better reflects their needs and wants. The companies which are likely to be successful in the future are those which adopt a more cooperative, participative style of management. People are important, and how they behave, grow and develop makes a difference to the success or failure of a company.

Managers of the future need to:

- encourage others to initiate ideas and solutions;
- share decision-making without giving up responsibility for results;
- apply and encourage creativity;
- listen as much as talk;
- delegate tasks, responsibility and authority;
- create cooperation in teams;
- create an environment of motivation and commitment;
- share information;
- develop employees;
- cope effectively with uncertainty, crisis and change;
- believe that the best solutions to problems may come from unexpected sources.

This is an interesting list for women, because of the similarities between the qualities on the list, and the qualities that are often considered to be characteristic of women.

Here is a list of accepted female strengths. Tick the characteristics you believe are important at work.

doing more than one task at the same time	☐
organising	☐
coping in crisis	☐
maintaining a wide awareness of situations and people	☐
accepting uncertainty	☐
making/changing priorities	☐
solving problems creatively	☐
using a gentler approach	☐
dealing with different types of people	☐
coping with change	☐
anticipating what needs to be done	☐
motivating people	☐
listening	☐
showing empathy	☐
'picking things up' (ie intuition)	☐
supporting others	☐
getting the job done	☐
understanding non-verbal communication	☐
getting to the point	☐
being tolerant of the opinions of others	☐
summarising quickly and concisely	☐
anticipating potential consequences	☐

Women can provide the flexible, innovative and creative approach which organisations seek. Indeed, women have an opportunity to draw upon the qualities of care, concern and intuition which have often been undervalued in the past.

Make sure that you recognise and promote the strengths that you have. They are an invaluable asset to your career.

3

Talks, Meetings and Interviews

Good managers are skilled at dealing with people — at all levels. Managers have ample opportunity to display these interpersonal skills on a daily basis during interactions with colleagues, subordinates and those outside the company. This chapter looks at these skills in-depth, with particular reference to preparing and giving talks and presentations, participating in meetings, and interviewing candidates for vacant posts.

TALKS AND PRESENTATIONS

For every talk or presentation you have sat through and enjoyed, there are probably ten others you cannot even remember. Perhaps you were bored or distracted, or even lost your way in a maze of jargon and technicalities. The ability to present information to an audience in a clear, confident and coherent way is one of the fundamental skills required in organisations today.

A good speaker:

- looks confident;
- keeps to the point;
- has interesting speech content and follows a logical order;
- is entertaining;
- does not speak in monotone;
- makes good use of visual aids;
- speaks clearly and simply;
- smiles and makes eye contact with different members of the audience;

- answers questions;
- does not overrun.

While all of these qualities are important, there is no doubt that you must *look* confident to speak well in public even if you do not really feel it! The secret is to be well prepared.

Preparation

Most experienced speakers freely admit that careful preparation is their secret. The more time you spend preparing, the more likely it is to go well. The following questions will help you prepare thoroughly:

Questions for preparing a talk

- What is the title of the talk?
- When will I be giving the talk?
- Why am I giving the talk?
- Who will my audience be?
- What final impression do I want them to have?
- How long will my talk last?
- What do I want to say?
- How will I say it?
- Where will I be giving the talk?

The next few pages consider these in detail.

As you work through the questions, complete the Talk preparation sheet which follows. Use an example of a talk/ presentation you have to give in the future, or one you have given in the recent past.

First, write the title of the talk at the top of the sheet over the page.

Talk preparation sheet

Title of talk

When will I be giving the talk?

Why am I giving the talk?	Who will my audience be?

What final impression do I want them to have?

How long will my talk last?

What do I want to say?

Key ideas	Key words	Visual aids
_____	_____	1.
_____	_____	2.
_____	_____	3.
_____	_____	4.
_____	_____	5.
_____	_____	6.
_____	_____	7.
_____	_____	8.
_____	_____	9.
_____	_____	10.

Where will I be giving the talk?

When will I be giving the talk?

Not only will the amount of preparation time affect any research you might want to carry out, but it will also affect the preparation of visual aids and the amount of practice time you can allow.

Why am I giving the talk?

Try to define your objective in a precise and concise sentence, against which you can test the material that you could include.

Who will my audience be?

What do they do for a living? What do they know about the subject already? What are their interests and concerns? To what level are they educated? Are they *Sun* or *Sunday Times* readers? You must find out about your audience to pitch your talk at the correct level.

What final impression do I want them to have?

What do you want them to do or think about, as a result of hearing your talk? It could be:

■ I'll buy one tomorrow.
■ This sounds really interesting — I think I'll go on that trip they are planning in two weeks.
■ We need to rethink this before making a decision.
■ We need to introduce a scheme like that in my company.

The last two questions may sound obvious, but too often they are overlooked as people rush to start the 'real' job of writing their speech. Some time spent thinking about the audience and the impression you want to leave them with, can make all the difference between your talk being memorable or forgettable!

How long will my talk last?

Find out the length of your 'slot' and do not forget to allow for questions. Remember, if you illustrate your talk with visual aids, the talk will take longer than you think it will. Being too brief is preferable to being too long, from the audience's point of view, although you must make sure that all the relevant information has been included.

Now return to your Talk preparation sheet and complete the following boxes:

■   *When will I be giving the talk?*
■   *Why am I giving the talk?*
■   *Who will my audience be?*
■   *What final impression do I want them to have?*
■   *How long will my talk last?*

The last question is the most difficult one.

What do I want to say?

You should aim to break your content down into six or seven key ideas which will form the framework for your presentation.

Let us take as an example a talk to persuade the owners of a small engineering company that they need and can afford an easy-to-use accounting software package. Seven key ideas would be the following:

1.   problems faced by small engineering companies;

2.   possible options;

3.   constraints;

4.   details of package;

5.   advantage over others;

6.   disadvantages;

7.   summary of reasons why they should buy.

The well-known sales adage, 'Tell them what you're going to tell them; tell them; then tell them what you've told them', is sound advice. The audience will always know where they are at each stage of the talk.

Before you fill in the framework, it is a good idea to show the key ideas to the person who asked you to do the talk. Sorting out the basics at this stage can save you much time and frustration later.

After you have your key ideas sorted out, you need to identify some key words for each idea. This will ensure that you keep your focus on the central issues. Look at this example for a software package:

Key idea	Key words
4. Details of package	price reliability comprehensive data easy to use

Complete the Key words section of your Talk preparation sheet.

Now you are ready to decide *how* you are going to present it.

How will I say it?

The two key questions here are the following:

1. Do I learn it or read it?

2. How do I make the best use of visual aids?

Speak it or read it?

Some people feel more confident writing out their speech in full and reading it. There are major problems with this approach, as there is a big difference between written and spoken English. If you read from a written document, it is likely to sound false and 'wooden'. If you are looking at the document you are reading, then you are not looking at your audience. They might start to wonder why they bothered to turn up! Your voice is unlikely to carry as well because your head will be lowered.

Try to get into the habit of talking rather than reading a speech. Use small cards, usually referred to as 'cue' cards, that you can hold and write your key ideas and words on. Number the points you want to make and put your key words in large letters or another colour. You can number your cue cards, or attach them together at one corner and just peel each one off as you finish your points.

Using visual aids

Preparing your data in an interesting and varied way avoids the risk of your audiences getting bored or losing concentration. It is also useful to include visual aids if you are nervous about attention being on you the whole time.

Seven key points about visual aids

1. Use them to explain, support or emphasise.

2. Consider all the visual aids available to you, from overhead projector transparencies, 35-mm slides, flip charts, blackboards, and whiteboards, to three-dimensional objects or models.

3. Use colour to make things clearer.

4. Keep visual aids simple — do not try to include too much information.

5. Link visual aids to aspects of your talk. Number each visual aid and write the number on the appropriate cue card.

6. If you use a slide or overhead projector, do not forget to switch it off when you are not using it, because the noise of the fan can be distracting; and do not forget to find out how it works *before* your presentation.

7. Provide copies of data for members of the audience,

if the numbers are not too large. Give them out at the end, or people may read the details rather than listen to you.

Now go back to your Talk preparation sheet and write down the visual aids you will use in your talk. Number them and write them next to the key word, also numbered, which will indicate at what point you are going to introduce them.

There is one more question you have to answer as part of your preparation.

Where will I be giving the talk?

If you can see the room you will be using beforehand, then you can check size, seating, lighting, heating, ventilation and access to electricity points. If you cannot visit the venue, make sure you know the address and exact route, and arrive in plenty of time to complete your preparations.

Now complete your Talk preparation sheet with the location.

The next stage comes between preparation and presentation and is essential, but it is one which is sometimes missed.

Practice

The importance of practising cannot be overemphasised. However good your preparation is, you will be judged on your actual performance. Practice can help you to control your nerves, thus controlling your voice.

Nervousness

Nerves affect different people in different ways. You may appear aggressive and speak much too loudly; your mouth may dry up making it difficult to swallow and breathe; your mind may go completely blank; you may feel unable to speak louder than normal for sustained periods; or you may speak far too quickly. One sure way your nerves will show is through your voice. If you can control your voice, you can control your nerves — or at least give that impression!

Voice control

There are three main ways to practise voice control, all of which will help you become familiar with the content of your presentation and get your timing right.

1. Practise on your own — in order to make sure you can see and use the key words on your cue cards; to find phrases and expressions which sound right for you; and to make sure you insert visual aids at the appropriate points.

2. Practise using a tape — to listen to your voice speed and make sure the pitch is right and to make sure your voice is not strained when you speak louder than usual.

3. Practise with a friend — to get feedback on content, visual aids, voice control and body language.

If you use any combination of the above, you will feel more confident when the time comes to deliver your talk.

Presentation

The effort you have made in preparing and practising your talk will go a long way to ensure that everything goes well on the day. However, there are certain things which can still go wrong and make the event entirely forgettable for your audience. Here are the most common problems and ways you can avoid them.

Improving presentation weaknesses

I never know what to do with my hands. It must be very irritating for the people I'm talking to.

Action points:

- Make sure that you hold something in your hands — cue cards or a pen.
- If you sit, keep your hands loosely together on your knee.
- If nervousness is causing you to wave your hands about, take some slow, deep breaths to calm yourself down before you start.

When I'm talking, I suddenly become aware that everyone's listening to me — then my mind goes completely blank.

Action points:

- If you have prepared well, you will have all the main points written on cue cards. A glance at the next one should bring you on to your next point immediately.
- Take a sip of water to buy yourself some time.

I haven't got a naturally loud voice and find it difficult to speak louder when I'm giving a talk.

Action points:

- Practise five minutes of your talk at a time in a louder voice than usual and gradually increase the time, until you can talk for half an hour without feeling strained.
- If feasible, use a microphone.

When I'm nervous I tend to speak too quickly, which can make it difficult for people to follow what I say.

Action points:

- Deliberately pause between each point you want to make.
- Consciously sit back (if you are in a chair!). It may help you to speak slower if you are more relaxed.

I know I can appear aggressive when I'm talking about something I feel strongly about, and this alienates my listeners.

Action points:

- A sign of aggression is using the hands forcefully and pointing. Hold your hands loosely or hold something.
- Adopt an open body posture to give out a friendly image.
- Lower your natural voice tone and speak slower.

I prefer to avoid eye contact with my listeners, so it's difficult to establish a rapport with them. I like to read out my written speech word for word.

Action points:

- Ask someone to observe where you do look — is it above an audience, or to one particular side, or at the person who nods at what you say?
- Practise eye contact in everything you do — when ordering a coffee in a café or having a team meeting.
- If speaking to an audience, make an effort to look at a different person every time you look up.

I find it difficult to relax in a formal setting, and I make others nervous too.

Action points:

- Use an open body posture.
- Smile and speak in a steady manner.
- Take some slow, deep breaths before you start.

I'm apprehensive about the questions at the end of the talk. I'm always afraid I'll be asked something I can't answer.

Action Points:

- Remember that you will probably anticipate the questions if you prepare your talk well.
- Prepare additional material if you think you might need it.
- Throw the question open and ask the audience for their comments.
- Use your cue cards, visuals, and diagrams for reference.
- Practise on a typical audience member to check if there are likely to be questions you have not thought of.
- If you do not know the answer, say so — but say you will find out or tell questioners where they could get the information.
- If you really do not feel comfortable, then it is perfectly reasonable to offer to discuss questions individually and informally after the presentation.

I'd rather not do it. I'm bound to make a fool of myself. Anyway, I haven't got anything interesting to say.

Action points:

- Most people hate giving presentations. Do not set yourself up to be perfect.
- Recognise that it is normal to feel anxious and tell yourself that you can control that by breathing correctly and taking sips of water.
- Remember that it does get easier with practice.
- Instead of telling yourself negative statements, try positive ones instead. You can! You shall! And do not apologise for anything!

Finally, here is some advice from one woman manager on how she handles presentations.

Case study

Briony Jones, Project Manager, Automobile Association, Basingstoke

If I'm doing a presentation, I try to do it in a way that encourages participation, or I structure it so I'm more facilitating rather than just telling people facts. I find that it works much better if people feel they have been brought into the discussion process and can affect the decisions that are being made. I do some presentation work; then pose questions for people to discuss among themselves and then obtain feedback. People don't expect this and find it alien at first but I explain that I'm trying to get their ideas in a structured way, with a real exchange of views — rather than one person just dominating the whole thing. I find this approach is generally appreciated.

MEETINGS

Good meetings do not just happen; they are made. The most ineffectual meetings are those which have no apparent purpose, those where no one speaks, and those which are badly chaired. In other words, meetings for meetings' sake. A meeting must have a clearly defined purpose; if it does not, it should never take place at all. The three main purposes of meetings are:

1.   to communicate information, eg team meetings;

2.   to solve problems, eg management meetings;

3.   to make decisions, eg strategy meetings.

Meetings are also a useful means of creating a sense of identity and cementing relationships in a team which may not meet on a day-to-day basis. They provide a structured forum for dissent and enable problems to be nipped in the bud.

Attenders who contribute positively place more value on the decisions which are made and have more commitment to their successful implementation. Meetings are a good way to brainstorm, as people share experiences and expertise. If handled properly, they can be motivating for staff and rewarding for managers.

As a manager, much of your time will be spent in meetings of one kind or another. It is in your interests to play your part in improving their effectiveness. As a woman, you may well be in the minority, and anything which you do or say will be scrutinised by the other participants. Your confidence and competence will be assessed on your behaviour during the meeting.

Being in the minority

Do any of these comments strike a chord with you?

> I was at a meeting to discuss the new building programme, and I happened to be the only woman there. At one point I expressed concern at the projected staffing levels and my comment was ignored. I knew it was a valid point because I'd discussed it with the planners.

> I attended a meeting with senior management where the main item on the agenda was a policy change that would affect working practices in my department. I opposed the change, and, although I knew that others felt the same as I did, I was the only one who voted in this way.

> I had to chair the meeting, as my boss was on leave. One of the other men didn't like this at all. He couldn't resist the temptation to be sarcastic and make me look foolish.

One of the problems of being a woman in a management position is that you may find yourself in a minority. This may put you at a disadvantage in a number of situations. Meetings are a good example of this. Here is a situation when women often find they are not taken seriously. It is often the case that he who shouts loudest and longest wins in the end, and women find it a struggle to make their voices heard in the same way.

A woman manager may find that the type of supportive behaviour that she would receive from other women, in allowing her to express her views, is lacking in a predominantly male atmosphere. This can be intimidating for many women, who may respond in one of two ways. Either they may remain silent, confirming their lack of worth (or interest) in the eyes of the male majority, or they may compensate for an apparent lack of power by behaving aggressively. Neither of these responses works. The woman concerned will be ineffectual in the meeting. Moreover, she will be *seen* to be ineffectual.

Think back to an occasion when you spoke at a meeting which was attended by men and women, and briefly describe any problems that you experienced in:

1. **speaking up;**

2. **putting forward your ideas for consideration;**

3. **influencing other people's opinions;**

4. **influencing the way the meeting progressed.**

1.

2.

3.

4.

What often happens is that men dominate the proceedings and have more success in making their opinions known and considered. But it does not have to be like that!

How to be effective in meetings

Firstly, you have a three-fold responsibility to be effective in meetings.

1. a responsibility to your staff to represent their interests and their views;

2. a responsibility to the other members of the meeting to ensure its effectiveness — everyone has a duty to participate;

3. a responsibility to yourself to promote opinions, ideas and needs which you believe to be important and worthy of consideration.

How can you be most effective? Here are some ideas.

Ten ways to be effective in meetings

1. Listen actively

Concentrate on what is being said — rather than on your response. Good listening leads to good questioning, improves group understanding, and keeps the meeting good-humoured.

Sometimes people prepare what they are going to say and then wait for an appropriate moment to intervene; consequently, they do not listen to other speakers. Participate fully in the discussion by listening actively. This is something which many people fail to do, and it leads to many misunderstandings — and much time-wasting.

If you feel that you need to prepare what you are going to say, jot down a few words on paper — and then tune in fully to what is being said.

2.   *Ask questions if you do not understand*

Women, in particular, are often misled into believing that everyone else (except them) understands what is going on. They may feel that by asking questions they are exposing ignorance, and that this displays vulnerability. There is no disgrace in asking for clarification of points which may be ambiguous or unclear. You will probably find that other people have been as unsure as you, if you ask: 'Are you saying that ...?' or 'What exactly do you mean by ...?'

Asking a question is also a useful way of gaining confidence — before coming in at a later stage to state your point of view.

3.   *Be confronting and supportive*

Many women dislike debate and argument because they feel that by opposing another person's point of view, they are rejecting that person. Remember that you have the *right* to state your viewpoint, even if it goes against those of other people at the meeting. Indeed, as a manager, you have a responsibility to participate on your own behalf, and on behalf of your staff.

Even if you disagree with what is being said, recognise and respect the right of other speakers to voice their point of view. Support does not have to be verbal — nods, smiles and other examples of non-verbal behaviour indicate agreement. When you wish to add the weight of your support to another speaker, do so:

- 'That's a good idea.'
- 'I agree with John when he said that ...'
- Although I can understand why you feel that way, I support Mary when she said ...'

Your support is thus likely to be appreciated, remembered and *reciprocated*.

4. *Speak clearly, honestly and directly*

When putting forward your own point of view do not be afraid of saying 'I'. Be more concerned with what you are saying than how other people are reacting to you. Try not to let anxieties about your behaviour affect the way in which you present your point of view. On the whole, people are less likely to be aware of your nerves than you think they are.

5. *Do not let others interrupt you*

It is easy to back down and stop speaking when you are interrupted, particularly if the other person is louder, aggressive, or more senior. What makes it perhaps more difficult is the fact that such intervention disrupts your mental flow, and you may lose your train of thought. Some people react to interruptions by continuing to speak, but louder. Others find it easier to draw attention to the interruption by asking to be allowed to continue.

In the same way, if you find it difficult to find a gap in the debate to put forward your point of view, try not to intervene by interrupting another speaker. Attract the attention of the chairperson to the fact that you wish to speak.

6. *Keep your contributions positive, short and to the point*

The people who achieve most at meetings are often those who say little but listen carefully, and who have planned their contribution. Much time is wasted in discussions by people who speak at length as a power ploy or in order to score points over another participant. You will appreciate the attempts made by other people to be brief and concise; therefore try to do so yourself.

7. *Use non-verbal communication to reinforce what you say*

When you speak in a meeting, pay attention to the manner

in which you speak and how you appear. A confident voice and demeanour will reinforce the impact of what you are saying. Note also the following points:

- Speak audibly.
- Vary the tone of your voice — you are more likely to hold people's attention this way.
- Do not smile when making a serious point — or laugh after you have made it.
- Stand up if you feel more confident — you will make more impact.
- Do not fidget — it distracts others from what you are saying.

8. Ask for a response to your contribution, if you do not get one

If you feel that your point has been glossed over, request a response:

- 'I feel that this is the case. Does this point of view have any support?
- 'How do other people feel about this suggestion?'
- 'I feel that the points I have made are worthy of consideration. Do I need to expand on them?'

9. Do not back down just because people do not accept what you say

If you do not have confidence in yourself, it is easy to be swayed by somebody else's point of view. Allow yourself some time to consider the merits of other people's arguments before rejecting your own.

10. Do not fall in with an apparent majority

Decide whether you feel it is important to make a stand on the issue. There may be pressure to make a quick — and maybe wrong — decision because of deadlines, impatience or influence by powerful members at the meeting. If you feel strongly about a particular issue, you may decide to hold out against the views of the majority.

In an attempt to ensure that your ideas prevail, you could:

- suggest that a final decision be delayed;
- add the topic to the next agenda;
- call a meeting of like-minded individuals;
- circulate your views for further consideration and comment.

It may just work — if you persevere!

Remember, there is no disgrace in changing your mind if you decide that you were not in full possession of the facts, having heard all the other points of view.

Now that you have read all the guidelines, were there any that made you think, 'Yes, that's something I must do in the future?'

Reread the guidelines and focus on any which you wish to remember and implement in order to become more effective at meetings.

How I can be more effective at meetings

If you managed to identify some things that you can do, make sure that you put them into practice at the next meeting you attend.

If you have never contributed very much in the past, take things slowly and remember that you are not suddenly going to change the habits of a lifetime overnight. When you have carried out one of your intentions, evaluate it afterwards. Ask yourself: 'How was I? How could I improve next time?' If you have a friend or colleague whom you can trust and rely upon for a fair opinion, ask this person to help you assess your performance.

If you feel that your contribution to meetings is good, positive and difficult to improve upon, ask yourself how you could help the meetings you attend to run more smoothly for everyone present. Bear in mind that, as with most things in life, what you get out of a meeting will usually be in direct proportion to what you put in. Like most skills, being effective in meetings does become easier with practice.

Meetings are an important forum for women to exercise influence, and to get themselves noticed. As a woman with her sights set on the next step of the promotional ladder, you should realise that meetings can play a key role in gaining you visibility, credibility and respect for your competence and confident behaviour. This is particularly the case if you are asked to chair a meeting.

Chairing a meeting

The success of a meeting largely depends upon the effectiveness of the person in the chair. It is not an easy role for anybody to take on, particularly if you have had little or no experience of being in this position. Consider the qualities of a good chairperson.

A good chairperson should:

- arrive on time and start the meeting promptly;
- state the purpose of the meeting and give a deadline for finishing;

- go through the items on the agenda in order of priority, giving a brief introduction to each;
- structure the time taken to discuss each issue;
- invite contributions from the floor;
- encourage brevity and stop any person from dominating the discussion;
- encourage participation from quieter attenders who, nevertheless, have skills and experience that the meeting can draw upon;
- put an end to any discussion which digresses too widely from the item being debated. If there is any digression, it should be discussed only with the permission of the members.
- listen carefully. By listening and responding, a good chairperson can help members to clarify their ideas. Good listening also helps to build an atmosphere of trust and understanding.
- remain neutral;
- ask questions to clarify and eliminate confusion and to steer the discussion in the right direction;
- ask 'long-winded' contributors to summarise what they are trying to say;
- watch the audience for reactions. Pay attention to non-verbal communication and try to bring any dissent into the open by the use of questions.
- allow constructive disagreement — without allowing the atmosphere to deteriorate;
- summarise the 'situation so far' from time to time and check for assent;
- ensure that full and accurate minutes are being recorded — by someone else;
- keep a sense of humour and even temper;
- give a brief summary at the end; agree deadlines for progress reviews; set date, time and place for the next meeting.

The length of the list indicates that being in the chair is a skilful job. Those who do it well make it look easy — those who do not can make it a torturous experience for those attending.

Evaluate meetings

Every attendee at a meeting is responsible for ensuring that time is used well and the objectives of the meeting are met. For the purpose of evaluating a meeting, there are three aspects to consider:

1. content — opinion, suggestions, information; expertise, etc.

2. process — putting arguments for and against prioritising, summarising, asking for contributions, setting deadlines, etc. 'Process' is concerned with giving a structure to the meeting.

3. feelings — frustration, boredom, anxiety, dissatisfaction, etc.

For each of these three elements of meetings, there are things that people do which can help or thwart the success of the meeting. If a meeting is to achieve its maximum effect, there should be a balance of all types of behaviour.

As a manager, it is important for you to improve your own performance in meetings, but also to play a key role in helping others contribute well. The best place to start is with your team. All members should contribute. To help you and your team do this, try the following exercise, with their cooperation.

Use the Check-list for evaluating meetings on page 80 in the following way:

1. **At the top of the columns, write the initials of all participants in your meeting.**

2. **During the meeting, every time a statement is made, place a tick below the participant's name in the appropriate column.**

3. **Afterwards, total the number of ticks for each person and each type of behaviour.**

4. **From the number of ticks under 'negative',**

identify the areas (content, process, feelings), people and types of behaviour which are causing problems.

5. From the number of ticks under 'positive', assess what was good about the meeting.

6. From the columns left blank under 'positive', consider what can be done to make the meeting more productive.

7. Ask yourself what you, as participant, chairperson or team leader, can do to achieve a better balance of all three important elements of meetings in the future.

Check-list for evaluating meetings

Positive							
stating point of view clearly, audibly and briefly							
listening actively							
asking questions							
supporting							
confronting constructively							
developing others' point of view							
asking for feedback on contribution							
giving information							
challenging assumptions							
giving clarification							
injecting humour							
starting on time							
defining the purpose							
putting an end to digressions							
summarising points							
monitoring progress							
prioritising items to be discussed							
inviting contributions							
encouraging brevity							
checking for assent							
ensuring that minutes are taken							
finishing on time							
arranging next meeting							
stimulating ideas							
expressing feelings							
asking how others feel							
exploring feelings							
acknowledging how others feel							

Negative							
making assumptions							
speaking too generally							
stating opinions as fact							
using sarcasm, put-downs, etc.							
mocking							
speaking for too long							
interrupting							
having private conversations							
muttering							
blocking							
not listening							
backing down unnecessarily							
insisting in the light of new information							
going off the topic							
changing the subject							
jumping ahead							
jumping back							
circling issues/skirting around the subject							
ignoring own feelings							
dismissing feelings of others							
not checking for feelings of others							

One way in which you could use this check-list is to ask one person to act as an observer and, having explained to the team the purpose of the exercise (if you wish to), get the observer to use the check-list in the way suggested. By doing this, you should be able to identify any negative behaviour which makes the meeting less productive. With encouragement and instruction from you and a commitment from the members of the team to contribute constructively, you should be able to improve the effectiveness of your meetings.

Here are some helpful comments from other women managers.

Case studies

Division director, Industrial Society, London

> It's essential to really do your homework. You have to be very sure of your facts and be capable of expressing them quickly and simply in a meeting. Recognise that getting your point of view across may be quite difficult. If you're in a minority with a group of men and they are choosing not to take you seriously — that's when knowing your facts really matters, as does having the ability to push your point home.

Finance manager, large manufacturing company

> Notes and research are important. If you're going to be arguing a point — you have to be sure of what you are saying. I like to be able to scan through my notes and say, 'Yes, but ...', and state the facts. I'm inclined to defend my corner rather strongly and quickly so I need to be a little more patient.

Jill Murkin, Training Manager, Marks and Spencer, London

> Be prepared to make your views known, and not to just sit back and let other people control the discussion. If you feel nervous about doing this, note down the points you wish to make. If you're attending a meeting, ensure you have a copy of the agenda and know what issues people are going to raise so that you won't be caught off guard by anything that is brought up during the meeting.

INTERVIEWS

Conducting an effective recruitment interview is an important role of management. There's no substitute for practice, but there are certain things you can do before, during and after the interview to ensure the process runs smoothly and that the best candidate is selected.

Before the interview

Recruiting new staff is an important job for a manager, because you will usually have to live with the results of your choice for quite some time. If a poor decision is made, the organisation is left with an unsatisfactory employee, and the repercussions of this person's performance can affect other team members.

Despite its proven fallibility in finding the right person for the job, the interview is still the most widely used method for selecting new staff. Yet, rarely is an interview regarded for what it is — an exchange of information and ideas in which both parties are 'buyers' and 'sellers'. The employer is looking to 'buy' loyalty, skills, and talent, and needs to 'sell' the benefits of working for that particular organisation. The candidate is looking to 'sell' qualities, skills, and experience, and is looking to 'buy' a challenging job accompanied by a list of benefits to match personal values.

The key to success, as with most things, lies in good preparation. You need to prepare:

- the job description;
- the person specification;
- the physical setting;
- the interview structure;
- the assessment system.

The job description

You need to assess what the job involves, and what tasks are to be performed. The job description must include:

- job title;
- grade (if relevant);
- location/place of work;
- main duties/tasks/responsibilities;
- whom the job holder is accountable to.

It can also include:

- physical conditions;
- pressures and satisfactions of the job;
- resources and support which are available;
- relationships to others outside and inside the organisation;
- benefits and prospects for promotion;
- limits of authority.

If somebody is to be appointed to your department, try to be closely involved from the start. Do not leave the business of drawing up a job description to Personnel — if you can have some input, then do so.

The person specification

The person specification aims to describe the type of person best suited to the job. This will include some or all of the following information:

- expertise;
- health;
- physical characteristics;
- general intelligence;
- educational skills;
- special skills;
- interests, attitudes, motivation;
- personal qualities;
- general circumstances — location of home, travel requirements etc.

When you consider the person specification, you must take into account all the qualities, characteristics and attributes which you think are necessary to do the job effectively. The care that is taken in the initial stages of the job hunt will save time, money and effort in the long term, as you begin to narrow down the list of suitable candidates.

With good jobs at a premium, organisations receive hundreds of applications for some of the posts they advertise. The discipline of writing out a job description and person profile will help you identify whom to reject, who may be worth seeing, and who is definitely worth seeing.

Once you have decided whom you wish to interview, you can then think about arrangements.

The physical setting

The ideal location for an interview is quiet, private and free from distractions such as staff interruptions or ringing telephones. On the morning of the interview, you should ensure that you have everything you need, and that the room is equipped and in order. Arrange to be undisturbed and, if the candidates are going to have to wait, provide some reading material for them to browse through. You might also like to make arrangements for refreshments to be served at some stage.

Decide in advance who will receive the candidates and brief this person on exactly what to do, what to say, and where to take the candidates. Ensure that every candidate is greeted and treated in exactly the same way. If you wish this person to provide an informal assessment of each candidate, let him or her know exactly what you are looking for.

The interview structure

The questions are the central part of the interview procedure and must be planned in advance. Knowing your structure will make you less likely to make an intuitive judgement during the opening stages. Prepare questions that you can ask *all* candidates in order that they have an equal opportunity to demonstrate their ability and suitability.

Twenty common interview questions

1.   Tell me about yourself.

2.   Why do you want this job?

3.   Will you accept this job if it is offered to you?

4.   What would you say were your main achievements in your present job?

5.   Why are you leaving your present job?

6.   What do you regard as your particular strengths?

7.   In what areas would you like to improve?

8.   What sort of career challenge are you looking for now?

9.   What can you offer to this organisation?

10. How would you change things here if you got the job?

11. What are your career plans?

12. How do you get along with other people?

13. Why have you had so many/so few jobs in the last few years?

14. What additional training have you had while working?

15. How do you think you will cope with your lack of experience in . . . ?

16. How will you cope with the drawbacks of . . . ?

17. How do you think your career to date has fitted you for this job?

18. Have you discussed this job with your husband/wife?

19. How would you deal with a situation such as this . . . ?

20. When will you be free to start?

If a candidate's responses do not tell you what you need to know, then follow up your initial question with more specific ones. Do not allow candidates to talk their way round a difficult question, or omit the detail you need.

Once you have worked out the questions, consider how long you have available, and allocate this time appropriately.

Finally, before the interview, you need to consider the following topic.

The assessment system

One way of assessing each candidate's performance is to go back to your person specification and give a rating, say, out of ten, for each area or for particular qualities within an area. Then work out a way of recording this. Often it is difficult to listen to what a person is saying as well as writing notes; thus, it may help if you mark the rating on a prepared table of qualities.

During the interview

During the interview you should aim to create an atmosphere which will encourage the candidates to talk and to show themselves to their best advantage. You can then make the best-informed decision, and the candidates will feel that they have been fairly treated and had ample opportunity to state their case.

Be friendly and relaxed yourself. Begin by introducing yourself and your job title, and explain how the interview will proceed. Explain the purpose of the interview. Provide some background information about the job and your organisation, but keep it brief.

On average, the interview should last from 20 to 40 minutes, although much will depend upon the level of the job. Do not dominate the proceedings because you feel uncomfortable when there is a silence. Your aim should be to let the candidate do at least 70 per cent of the talking. You will find out what you need to know only by listening to what is said to you. Candidates find interviews stressful and may try to cover their nervousness by talking too much. If this happens, you can thank them and say: 'That tells me all I need to know about that. Let's now move on to ...'

As far as possible, use 'open questions', that is, questions which cannot be answered by a simple 'yes' or 'no'. By asking open questions, you can encourage the candidate to talk freely about opinions, ideas, feelings and attitudes. Here are some examples.

- 'How did you feel when ...?'
- 'If you had to deal with a situation in which ... what would you do?'
- 'What happened when ...'
- 'What do you mean when you say ...?'
- 'Can you give me an example of ...?'
- 'I'd like to hear more about ...'
- 'What did you find interesting about ...?'
- 'What was it about ... that particularly appealed to you?'

When the candidate has answered your questions, summarise what has been said. This provides a structure to the interview, and lets the person know that you have been listening. You can assess candidates' motivation by getting them to tell you what they did and why they did it. People with high aspirations who have consistently achieved what they set out to do are obviously well motivated. People who have suffered setbacks and overcome them have more drive than those who have not made the most of opportunities they have had in the past. Well-motivated people will probably ask questions about training or career development, indicating that they are keen to improve and to expand their role.

At the end of the interview, shake hands, thank the interviewees for coming, and explain when and how they will hear from you.

After the interview

Allow yourself time before coming to a decision. The most systematic way of doing this is to use a rating system. This helps to avoid the common fault of coming to a conclusion during the first four minutes, or basing your decision on one positive or one negative aspect of an interviewee's performance. Make sure that you weigh up the pros and cons of each candidate before making the final decision.

The secret of being a good interviewer comes down to sound preparation and plenty of practice. But practice is no good unless you review your own performance each time, and learn something from it. To help you to do this, the following 'Interviewer's evaluation check-list' can be used to assess and improve your own performance. You may find the guidelines useful for other forms of interviews such as appraisal, counselling and review.

Interviewer's evaluation check-list

Did I?

- ☐ Ensure that the interview room was:
  - ▪ quiet
  - ▪ private
  - ▪ comfortable
  - ▪ interruption-free
  - ▪ equipped as necessary
- ☐ Arrange the candidate's reception
- ☐ Brief the person to receive them
- ☐ Prepare my questions in advance
- ☐ Allocate my time
- ☐ Work out an assessment system
- ☐ Create a relaxed atmosphere for the candidate
- ☐ Achieve a good rapport
- ☐ Start the interview well
- ☐ Listen more than I talked
- ☐ Use open questions to elicit information
- ☐ Follow up leads
- ☐ Give the candidate my complete attention
- ☐ Control the interview well
- ☐ Allow the candidate time to ask questions
- ☐ Summarise what the candidate said to make sure I got it right
- ☐ Smile and use non-verbal communication in an encouraging way
- ☐ End the interview well
- ☐ Allow enough time
- ☐ Consider carefully the merits of the candidate

4
Dealing with the Pressures

The stresses and strains of modern life are well documented. More than 50 per cent of illnesses reported to GPs are stress-related, and more working days are lost through this type of illness than through industrial disputes. As a manager, you have to learn to recognise and deal with your own stress in order to work effectively. You may also find that the stress experienced by your staff becomes your problem too, if it starts to affect behaviour and performance at work.

This chapter gives you the opportunity to identify your own pressure points — both positive and negative. It looks at some short-term ways of coping and a long-term strategy you can employ.

PRESSURE — THREAT OR CHALLENGE?

Pressure is not intrinsically harmful. Pressure can provide challenge and stimulus, enabling people to mobilise their resources in order to get things done. Not everyone performs better under pressure, but most people can withstand a certain amount and respond positively when the need arises.

Consider an event or activity in your life which you personally have found exhilarating and challenging.

A source of positive pressure for me is:

What did you choose? A sport, a social event, working to tight deadlines, competition, or perhaps Christmas or planning a holiday?

In the check-list overleaf, tick the ways in which you respond positively to pressure. The blank spaces at the end are for you to write in your own positive response.

Positive responses to pressure

When I am under pressure, I:

- ☐ work better
- ☐ work more quickly
- ☐ am more creative
- ☐ take more risks
- ☐ accomplish more
- ☐ am on a 'high'
- ☐ look good
- ☐ have lots of energy
- ☐ feel important
- ☐ am more assertive
- ☐ put myself first
- ☐ can fight illness
- ☐ am more confident
- ☐ have more authority
- ☐ am more enthusiastic
- ☐
- ☐
- ☐
- ☐

If you found that you were able to tick even a few of these positive responses, you are obviously the sort of person who reacts well to pressure.

If you are the sort of person who performs less well under pressure, do not worry — you are not alone. There are plenty of people who find that pressure affects them adversely; in other words, the pressure becomes stress. What matters most is that you are aware of the causes, effects and ways of controlling the pressure in your life. Awareness is 90 per cent of the solution, and you will look at some solutions later in this chapter.

At what point does 'pressure' become 'stress'? 'Pressure' is an external stimulus, while 'stress' is a negative reaction to pressure when it is too difficult to control. Stress is readily definable for most people. It includes:

- being overloaded;
- feeling completely exhausted;
- being mentally and physically fatigued;
- feeling unable to cope;
- having too much to do in too little time;
- not being able to function normally;
- feeling physical, emotional or mental discomfort;
- being depressed.

The negative effects of this stress can show up through unsuitable behaviour, low energy and performance levels, and, ultimately, poor health.

Read the list of stress 'symptoms' over the page and tick the ones that most often apply to you. Add any of your own to the bottom of the list.

Stress symptoms

When I feel stressed, I:
- ☐ drop things
- ☐ make incorrect decisions
- ☐ cannot concentrate
- ☐ shout more than usual
- ☐ work badly
- ☐ have quick mood changes
- ☐ have backache or neck ache
- ☐ cry
- ☐ have difficulty in falling asleep
- ☐ smoke more
- ☐ eat more
- ☐ go off my food
- ☐ make excuses to avoid doing things
- ☐ make excuses to avoid people
- ☐ concentrate on trivial things
- ☐ feel tired easily
- ☐ drink too much alcohol
- ☐ have nightmares
- ☐ feel sorry for myself
- ☐ sleep more
- ☐ nag
- ☐ talk too much
- ☐ lose things

want to be left alone	☐
have gynaecological problems	☐
feel unwell	☐
have cystitis	☐
have more painful periods	☐
cannot have sex	☐
lie awake in the night	☐
wake early in the morning	☐
want to give up work	☐
find fault with other people	☐
scrub the floor	☐
worry about trivial things	☐
take time off work	☐
make a lot of mistakes	☐
perspire	☐
have headaches	☐
shake	☐
cannot get up in the morning	☐
feel dizzy	☐
forget things	☐
twitch	☐
want to escape	☐
want to be with friends	☐
	☐
	☐

By now, you should have identified some of the ways in which your body and your mind react to stress.

Some of these symptoms appear immediately; others gradually appear when stress builds up over a long period. Not everyone reacts in the same way to stress, because people have varying abilities to cope.

Your capacity to cope

The degree to which you are able to cope with a potential source of stress depends upon several things.

- Your culture — some events are more stressful in some societies than in others.
- Your past experience — the way in which you responded to a similar situation in the past may well have a bearing upon your reaction next time.
- Your physical well-being — your ability to tolerate stress will be affected by the state of your health. Diet, exercise and sleep can all help or hinder your efforts to cope.
- The amount of support you have — it can help to relieve the burden and find a solution to the problem if you share your feelings with others.
- Other demands being made upon you at the same time — the more 'stressors' there are upon you, the more difficulties you will have in trying to deal with them.
- Your perception of yourself — if you regard yourself as the sort of person who can cope with most things, you have a better chance of being able to cope in reality.
- Your lifestyle — in general, the more roles and responsibilities you have, the greater the chance that you will suffer from stress.
- Your personality — the negative effects of stress are often found to be associated with people who are described as having 'Type A' characteristics. Moreover, research has shown that the majority of women managers are in this category. Type A people are said to suffer from 'hurry sickness' and to do everything fast — eat, walk, speak and move.

Tick the statements which apply to you.

Type 'A' personality characteristics

I hate being late.	☐
I do not like losing at anything.	☐
I become impatient when other people are talking, and often finish their sentences for them.	☐
I am always in a hurry.	☐
I find it hard to relax.	☐
I feel guilty when I have nothing particular to do.	☐
I talk loudly and quickly.	☐
I interrupt people when they speak.	☐
I do not suffer fools gladly.	☐
I drive fast and become impatient with slower drivers.	☐
I do not listen when others are talking.	☐
I do not have many interests outside work.	☐
I often do two things at the same time.	☐
I am very ambitious and do not let others stand in my way.	☐
I try to get other people to do things more quickly.	☐
I am often aggressive when people exasperate me.	☐
I worry a lot about things — and people — I cannot control.	☐
I work long hours.	☐
I find it difficult to unwind on holiday.	☐
I have high demands of myself and of those I work/live with.	☐

Although this is a somewhat crude way of assessing your Type A characteristics, it nevertheless gives some indication of your degree of 'hurry sickness'. In general, the more of these statements that you tick, the more likely you are to suffer from stress.

- Under 5 — the risk is not high.
- 5 to 10 — you show some characteristics of Type A behaviour.
- 10 plus — you are probably a Type 'A' personality.

The first step towards minimising the effects of stress is to recognise the stress, as well as your own personality characteristics. What matters most is your perception of the event. You cannot change your culture or past experiences; nor change personalities at a whim. However, you can adjust perceptions, behaviour and lifestyle to adapt more easily to the stress.

As a manager, you have an obligation to make these changes — an obligation to the organisation, colleagues and staff, but, most of all, to yourself.

SOURCES OF STRESS

Before looking at some ways of managing stress, what are the causes, or sources, of it? For most people, the cause of stress is either work-related or due to events which happen in their lives.

Events

In a major piece of research carried out by two US doctors, Thomas Holmes and Richard Rahe, the degree of stress caused by specific events was assessed. The findings are reproduced on the following pages.

EVENT	SCORE
1. Death of spouse	100
2. Divorce	73
3. Marital separation from mate	65
4. Detention in jail or other institution	63
5. Death of a close family member	63
6. Major personal injury or illness	53
7. Marriage	50
8. Being fired at work	47
9. Marital reconciliation with mate	45
10. Retirement from work	45
11. Major change in the health or behaviour of a family member	44
12. Pregnancy	40
13. Sexual difficulties	39
14. Gaining a new family member (eg through birth, adoption, oldster moving in, etc)	39
15. Major business readjustment (eg merger, reorganisation, bankruptcy, etc)	39
16. Major change in financial state (eg much worse off or much better off than usual)	38
17. Death of a close friend	37
18. Changing to a different line of work	36

EVENT	SCORE
19. Major change in the number of arguments with spouse (eg either many more or many fewer than usual regarding child-rearing, personal habits, etc)	35
20. Taking on a mortgage (eg purchasing a home, business, etc)	31
21. Foreclosure on a mortgage or loan	30
22. Major change in responsibilities at work (eg promotion, demotion, lateral transfer)	29
23. Son or daughter leaving home (eg marriage, attending college, etc)	29
24. In-law troubles	29
25. Outstanding personal achievement	28
26. Wife beginning or ceasing work outside the home	26
27. Beginning or ceasing formal schooling	26
28. Major change in living conditions (eg building a new home, renovation, deterioration of home or neighbourhood)	25
29. Revision of personal habits (dress, manners, associations, etc)	24
30. Troubles with the boss	23
31. Major change in working hours or conditions	20
32. Change in residence	20

EVENT	SCORE
33. Changing to a new school	20
34. Major change in usual type and/or amount of recreation	19
35. Major change in church activities (eg much more or less than usual)	19
36. Major change in social activities (eg clubs, dancing, visiting, etc)	18
37. Taking on an hp agreement, or loan (eg purchasing a car, TV, freezer, etc)	17
38. Major change in sleeping habits (much more or much less sleep, or change in part of day when asleep)	16
39. Major change in number of family get-togethers (eg many more or many fewer than usual)	15
40. Major change in eating habits (much more or much less food intake, or very different meal hours or surroundings)	15
41. Vacation	13
42. Christmas	12
43. Minor violations of law (eg traffic tickets, jaywalking, disturbing the peace, etc)	11

Journal of Psychosomatic Research, Vol 11, 1967.

Use the life events rating scale to assess the level of stress which you have experienced during the past year. Identify those events on the list which apply to you and total your score.

My life events score for the past year is ☐

How much stress have you been under? Compare your score with the assessments given below:

Score	Assessment
Below 60	Your life is unusually free of stress.
60–80	A normal amount of stress.
80–100	Rather high stress.
100 +	You are under serious stress.

The life events rating scale for stress is an interesting exercise which may have highlighted some of your own problems. Before you place too much importance in these findings, however, note that this piece of research may not be directly applicable to you in particular, or women in general. It was carried out on male personnel in the US, and the weighting given to each event reflects the lifestyles of these particular men.

As stated earlier, an identical situation may have a different effect on different people, and the same event may affect the same person in different ways, depending upon other factors operating at the time. Problems tend to arise when more than one of these events happen at the same time. There are only so many changes you should make in your life at any one time. It may be making matters worse if you also have a source of pressure at work to contend with.

Work

As most people spend a large percentage of their time at work, problems there can be a major and diverse source of stress. The problem areas can include:

- The nature of the job — the type of work, the amount of work and the level of responsibility.
- The organisation — the work ethic and culture, particularly if there is a conflict between company and personal goals. This can also include inadequate resources, unrealistic objectives and a lack of employee involvement.
- Career development — the intense competition for promotion and the additional responsibilities of a new role, particularly for a woman, who may have to combat prejudice and discrimination as well.
- Roles — the higher up the ladder you climb, the more stressful the job is likely to be, especially if work objectives are unclear or non-existent.
- Relationships at work — conflicts with colleagues, subordinates and senior management, particularly if your style of management differs from that of your predecessor.

In addition, it seems there are more sources of stress for women managers, than for men.

Sources of stress for women

Women embarking on a management career face not only the same sources of stress as male managers, but additional ones too. In research carried out on the problems faced by women managers, Marilyn Davidson and Cary Cooper isolated a number of factors which women in management tend to find particularly stressful:

- They receive less training in management than men.
- They are subjected to double standards — women are 'pushy' or 'bossy'; men are 'leaders'.

- They have few role models to follow, and those who have managed to achieve promotion are often isolated and unsure of themselves.
- They have difficulty in being assertive and lack confidence.
- They have multiple roles and responsibilities because of their home/work situation.

Here are three examples of the types of problems that can cause stress for women managers.

Case studies

Joan

Joan had reached the age of 30 without making any firm decision about having a family. She worked for a publishing company in a job that was very demanding in terms of time and energy. She began to feel the pressure of her advancing years and started to agonise over whether to have a child and how she was to take care of it. She did not feel she could cope with both a child and her present job, yet she enjoyed the stimulus and income that her job brought.

What made the pressures all the more difficult to bear was the fact that her husband had left the final decision to her, feeling that endless discussions about it were fruitless. Furthermore, she was suffering from the disapproval of her mother, who felt that the question of what she should do was obvious — 'settle down to raise a family'. The feeling of being in limbo was reducing her effectiveness at work. Because of the stress that she was under, Joan felt that maybe she should put off the decision until next year ...

Dee

Although she was well regarded by staff and colleagues at work, Dee felt that she did not receive the support and encouragement she needed from her immediate boss. He expected her to perform well, and she had never let him down.

There was to be some reorganisation in the company she worked for, and in preparation for these changes, everyone was to go before a panel for a performance appraisal. The thought of this gave Dee panic attacks, particularly because she realised that a number of new senior posts were in the pipeline. She had heard her boss talking about the suitability of two of her (male) colleagues for these posts, but there had been no mention of her name. She thought about looking for another job where her loyalty and good work would be appreciated ...

Sharon

Sharon worked as unit head in charge of a team of five. She was responsible for her own workload and for monitoring her staff. She had problems with one of the male members of her team, who felt that he was better qualified to do the job than she. He ignored her instructions and did things his way.

When Sharon tackled him about this, she was accused of 'nagging'. Her next tactic was to ignore his obstructiveness in the hope that it would cease. This did not seem to work either, and caused further problems with the team, who felt he was being unfairly favoured. This source of stress, on top of the others attendant on her role as unit head, was becoming more than she could bear ...

What are your sources of stress at work?

To see where your sources of stress at work lie, tick the statements on the following pages that are true for you.

List of sources of stress at work

The job
- [ ] Serious consequences if mistakes are made
- [ ] Unpleasant working conditions
- [ ] Excessive travel at work
- [ ] Working to tight deadlines
- [ ] Excessive travel to and from work
- [ ] Irregular hours/shifts
- [ ] Too much work to do
- [ ] Too little work to do
- [ ] Underqualified for work I am doing
- [ ] Overqualified for work I am doing

Roles
- [ ] No clear objectives
- [ ] Others not clear what I do
- [ ] Various demands for my time in conflict with each other
- [ ] Conflict between my unit and other units
- [ ] My work depends on the efficiency of other departments
- [ ] Management misunderstands the real needs of my department
- [ ] New priorities are constantly being introduced
- [ ] Decisions or changes affecting me are made without my knowledge or involvement
- [ ] I spend my time fighting fires instead of working to a plan
- [ ] My responsibilities overlap with other people's

Relationships

I have forgotten differences of opinion with my boss ☐
I get feedback only if my work is unsatisfactory ☐
My boss has favourites ☐
My boss does not support me ☐
I have difficulty in giving negative feedback ☐
I have difficulty in dealing with aggressive people ☐
I have difficulty in dealing with passive people ☐
I avoid conflict with my boss ☐
I avoid conflict with my colleagues ☐
I have no one at work to share my work problems with ☐

Career development

The threat of redundancy is always present ☐
There are few opportunities to move up ☐
My job is no longer challenging ☐
I am getting too old to promote ☐
My skills are very specialised ☐

The organisation

Decisions are usually made without employee participation ☐
My personal needs are in conflict with those of the organisation ☐
Administrative policies inhibit getting the job done ☐
Procedures are conflicting ☐
My professional expertise contradicts organisational practice ☐
Allocation of resources seems arbitrary ☐
There is little interdepartment communication ☐
Creative thinking is not encouraged ☐
Good performance is not rewarded ☐
Lines of responsibility are unclear ☐

Image

- ☐ How I see myself is different from how I see a female executive
- ☐ Others do not see me as a female executive
- ☐ I am expected to adopt a female executive role that is unnatural to me
- ☐ My boss's image of a female executive is different from mine
- ☐ I find it difficult to be assertive
- ☐ I am expected to be aggressive
- ☐ I am very critical of my own performance at work
- ☐ I have difficulty in standing up to my male boss
- ☐ I have difficulty in standing up to my male colleagues
- ☐ I am uncomfortable in the position of boss

Male boss

- ☐ My male boss feels threatened by me
- ☐ I have to work harder than anyone else to prove myself
- ☐ I have to work hard all the time to live up to my boss's expectations of me
- ☐ My boss uses my competence for his own advancement
- ☐ My individual talents are unnoticed because they are fused with my boss's
- ☐ If I perform to the best of my ability, I will show my boss up

Female boss

My female boss is very intimidating ☐

My personal style is very different from my female ☐
boss's

My female boss does not give me any extra help ☐
because she did not get any

My female boss does not want competition from ☐
other females

My female boss has adopted a male style of ☐
management

Male colleagues

My male colleagues see me as a threat ☐

My male colleagues see me as a token woman and ☐
resent my appointment

My male colleagues exclude me from what is going on ☐

My male colleagues treat me very coolly ☐

My male colleagues sexually harass me ☐

My male colleagues treat me as a sister/wife/ ☐
daughter, not as a manager

My male colleagues do not take me seriously ☐

My male colleagues do not support me ☐

Blocked promotion

- ☐ You have to be prepared to relocate to get on
- ☐ The management does not promote women to the top because it fears the reaction of male subordinates
- ☐ You have to go abroad to get on, and management does not send women abroad
- ☐ There is no career-break scheme
- ☐ Women returning to work after having a family operate at a lower level
- ☐ There are few/no part-time managers
- ☐ Training courses are usually off-site and last for a few days
- ☐ Women who have families are not treated as serious promotion candidates
- ☐ Management does not like the women bosses appointed in the past; therefore it will not promote any more
- ☐ Management promotes those in its own image, ie male

The wonder-woman syndrome

- ☐ I have most of the responsibility for running the home
- ☐ I feel guilty if I am home late
- ☐ I work extra hard at being a good mother to make up for the time I am at work
- ☐ I have to prove to myself that I am a super partner/ super mother/super manager
- ☐ I have to prove to others that I am a super partner/ super mother/super manager
- ☐ I am always justifying that the family does not suffer because I work
- ☐ I have no/hardly any time to myself
- ☐ I feel people are waiting for me to say, 'I can't cope'
- ☐ If the house does not run perfectly, I get the blame
- ☐ If the house does not run perfectly, I accept the blame

Lack of support

My partner expects me to run the house as well as work ☐

My partner is threatened by my success ☐

My partner considers his job more important than mine ☐

The family do not take my work seriously ☐

There are few women at work I can talk to about work problems ☐

My friends do not want to talk about my work ☐

I need more help in the house ☐

My family would prefer me not to work ☐

My partner does not expect to be inconvenienced because I work ☐

I meet few women in positions similar to mine ☐

You have probably cited some problems which will be felt
by some of your male colleagues, and others which are
specifically female. What can you do about these problems?
How can you control the stress in your life? You need to
deal with the short-term problems immediately, and then
find a strategy which is effective for you in the long term.

REACH FOR A STRATEGY

Strategies for dealing with stress depend very much on the
nature of the stress and whether it is a long-term or short-
term problem. Here are some of the short-term measures
that people adopt for coping with stress.

Ways of coping

Most people have very many resources for dealing with the
stress in their lives. Scream and shout, disappear, take a hot
bath — the methods are diverse, and sometimes unique.
What do you do?

If you do any of these things, tick the appropriate
boxes. The spaces at the bottom are for you to add
your own personal ways of coping.

Ways of coping with stress

shouting or screaming ☐

having a bath ☐

having a massage ☐

taking exercise ☐

spending some time alone ☐

listening to music ☐

having a cigarette ☐

having an alcoholic drink ☐

socialising ☐

relaxing ☐

treating myself ☐

throwing things ☐

physical contact — cuddling my partner ☐

laughing ☐

ironing ☐

indulging myself: eating, spending money ☐

writing down what is bothering me ☐

phoning a friend ☐

stroking the cat ☐

making a cup of tea/coffee ☐

putting the problem to the back of my mind ☐

crying ☐

☐

☐

Now ask yourself how well your chosen methods work? The fact is that some work, and some do not. Indeed, some of the methods to relieve stress may actually aggravate it in the long term. The methods which can aggravate the problems are associated with denial, escape and displacement.

Denial

Sometimes people refuse to accept that they are under stress because they cannot face the reality of having to do something about it. Denying that the problem exists may be a desperate attempt to drive it away, but failing to tackle it makes the problem worse. If you refuse to acknowledge that there is a problem, you repress the feelings which are associated with it. The fact that expressing your feelings is socially unacceptable makes the situation worse for someone in a responsible management position, particularly if the manager is female, and therefore automatically labelled 'emotional', 'neurotic', and 'not cut out for the job'. In fact, repressing feelings can lead to depression and even physical illness.

Escape

Smoking, drugs and alcohol are three examples of this kind of temporary relief which many people resort to when they feel under stress. All of these can easily lead to other problems which aggravate the original source of stress. Although people often think that there is little they can do other than 'escape and forget', there are more effective methods of seeking escape.

Displacement

'Displacement' occurs when people who are suffering from stress cause others to feel stressed too. Their efforts to cope are at the expense of those around them. Instead of confronting and tackling the source of stress, they redirect it to those they are working or living with. This method of coping has destructive implications for the organisation they work for. Those who behave in this way have little awareness of their own stress or of the effect that it has on those around them.

Some short-term methods of coping which are more likely to be successful are discussed below.

Distraction

Distraction means acknowledging that the problem exists, but taking yourself away from it for a while in order to restore your peace of mind. Examples of distraction from the list include 'taking some form of exercise', 'having a massage', and 'spending some time alone'. Distraction is a form of temporary relief which can improve your capacity to tackle the problem by restoring your physical and mental fitness.

Self-care

You need to make yourself a priority in order to be in the right state of physical and mental health to be able to cope. It helps if your lifestyle incorporates ways of doing this over the long term; but there are short-term measures that you can adopt, such as relaxing, spending some time on your own, or treating yourself to something nice.

Emotional release

This means 'letting off steam' by channelling rage, frustrations and pent-up feelings into a harmless pursuit. If you think of yourself under stress as a pot boiling over, you can help the situation a little by draining off some of the contents of the pot. Release your emotions by doing what comes naturally — cry, laugh, thump a cushion, iron away furiously or speak to a friend. All of these methods, and others, help some people sometimes.

If you have discovered from what you have read that the methods you use to relieve stress in the short term are effective and not harmful to you or to others, carry on using them. If you have found that there are more ways than you had considered previously, select a few that may work for you from the list which follows.

The following list of short-term methods of coping have worked for many people and may work for you. Select some that you can try in the future, and make them part of your action plan, which comes at the end of this volume.

Effective ways of coping with stress: short-term

Distraction

- cooking
- reading a good book
- decorating
- painting
- sewing/knitting/embroidery
- walking the dog
- cycling
- playing tennis
- doing the washing
- polishing
- watching TV
- making plans
- sorting out your clothes/a room/a cupboard
- doing something new — a new recipe, a new interest, a new friend

Self-care

- yoga
- listening to music
- day-dreaming
- taking a nap
- meditating
- relaxing
- having a massage/sauna
- taking a short break or holiday

- eating more slowly
- eating natural foods
- buying something new
- having a facial/hair-do
- going for a special meal
- spending some time alone
- reading a magazine
- seeing a friend

Emotional release

- crying
- ironing
- laughing
- thumping a cushion
- keeping a diary
- writing a letter
- phoning a friend
- swearing
- ripping up something
- playing a vigorous sport
- dancing
- singing
- acting
- cleaning the kitchen floor
- writing poetry

REACH Strategy

Learning how to manage your stress in the long term has to be a planned process, not a 'fast fix'. The first step is to accept that there is something that you can do. The longer you go without taking action, the more likely you are to damage your health, and the more difficult it will be to control the stress.

This is *your* opportunity to take action by applying a stress management technique called the 'REACH Strategy'. The REACH Strategy is as follows:

- Recognise and release;
- Evaluate;
- Accept;
- Confront;
- Happy.

Each one of these words represents a step in identifying a way of coping with your own stressor.

RECOGNISE the symptoms and source; RELEASE your feelings

The first thing you must do is to recognise that you are under stress. Acknowledge that the stress exists, and then go on to investigate its cause. One element in acknowledging the stress is to release your feelings. There are ways of doing this which are harmless and useful in restoring your equilibrium.

EVALUATE your options

Consider the options that are open to you. Ask yourself: 'What can I do about this particular situation?' There is usually more than one way of solving a difficult situation. You may need to get somebody else's perspective on the problem, particularly if it is one that has been bothering you for some time. Do not expect another person to make the decision for you, but talking through a problem with an interested listener often helps to clarify your own thoughts.

Then assess the consequences of each of the options which are open to you. Ask yourself: 'What is the worst thing that can happen if I take this action?' Next you decide on one of the following options.

ACCEPT

1.   There are some things in your life that you *can* change — if you want to.

Ask yourself whether you can change the situation that is causing you stress. Perhaps there is a solution that you know you will have to face eventually, but you keep delaying the inevitable. You have the right to make decisions for yourself and have the responsibility to accept the consequences.

2. There are some things in life you *cannot* change — even if you try.

You can either learn to accept the things that you cannot change or be continually upset about them. When you realise what is truly beyond your control, you can begin to accept the inevitable.

3. There are some things in your life that you may *not* *want* to change.

The consequences of making some changes may be less acceptable than keeping things as they are — despite the stress. This does not mean that you cannot do anything to minimise the effects, but you may have to defer the action that would eliminate the particular cause of stress.

If you decide that there is a course of action that you can take, the next step is confrontation.

CONFRONT the problem — or the person

Confronting the problem may involve changing your perception of the situation, or saying or doing something specific to relieve the stress. You have to:

■ choose the best of the options open to you;
■ write down your objectives — what you want to achieve;
■ draw up a time-scale — when you intend to start;
■ communicate to other people what you intend to do.

Confronting the problem may involve your having to face and speak to the person who is causing you stress. You will have to explain your feelings and how you would like to change the situation that exists between you at present.

Remember to speak in terms of 'I' rather than 'you'; the other person is less likely to feel threatened in this way, while positive and direct expression is likely to have most impact.

The final step in dealing with the stress is to implement your strategy, and then ask yourself the question that follows below.

HAPPY with the outcome?

If you have found a strategy which works for you, use it again. If not, then go back to REACH. Go through the steps again and modify or change your approach. You may think, this sounds fine in theory, but how does it work in practice? This is how it worked for the three women you read about earlier.

Case studies

Joan

Joan eventually realised that there were three separate decisions to be made:

1. whether or not to have a child;
2. if the answer was yes — how to care for the child and whether to carry on in her present job;
3. if the answer was no — what career plans should she make.

She had originally confused the issues by trying to decide on all three things simultaneously.

After weighing up all the options that were open to her, Joan decided that she was more committed to her career than to the idea of having a family. She told this to her husband and he supported her decision. The next problem was to tackle her mother, whose initial reaction was one of disbelief. Joan accepted that her mother would probably never come to terms with the decision that she had made, but refused to allow herself to be manipulated by other people's expectations of her.

Dee

Dee recognised that she had two sources of stress:

1.   the forthcoming appraisal interview;

2.   the lack of support from her boss.

Therefore, she made up her mind to tackle them separately.

In order to reduce her anxieties for the interview, she assessed her strengths and weaknesses, and planned how she was going to promote her skills for the post that she was seeking. Having done some preparation, she felt more at ease about her ability to cope with any questions she might be asked.

Secondly, she chose her time and place carefully, and went over in her mind what exactly she was going to say to her boss. She explained to him that she did not feel he gave her the support that she deserved. His reaction was one of surprise, and he said that he had not realised she felt that way or that she was interested in promotion. He had always been satisfied with her work and was prepared to support her application for a more senior post.

Although Dee felt that her boss thought she was a bit neurotic for saying what she did, she was relieved at having expressed her feelings openly, and this helped to reduce her stress. She would not be as hesitant if a similar situation arose again.

Sharon

Sharon realised that the stress she felt was caused partly by her inability to face the situation. She accepted that she had to improve the performance of the 'problem male' and restore her credibility with the team.

She confronted the situation by arranging to speak to the person who was causing her problems. She explained how she felt about his attitude and general obstructiveness and gave him the opportunity to voice any resentment he felt at her being given the promotion. Having 'cleared the air' in this way, Sharon then went on to spell out what she expected of him in terms of performance. Standards were set down and agreed by both of them, to be reviewed at a future date.

Although the relationship between them continued to be strained, she had regained the respect of the rest of the team by tackling the problem in this way — and removed at least one source of stress at work.

Now you are going to use the 'REACH Strategy' to identify a solution that may work for you, using the questions as a guideline.

REACH Strategy

What is your current source of stress which you want to change?

What are your options for dealing with this situation? List them all, no matter how extreme.

1.

2.

3.

4.

What is your best option?

What are you going to do or say to confront the situation?

When are you going to do this?

When you have put your strategy into practice, record the results here.

Were you happy with the way it worked?

Answer the next two questions only if the strategy did not work as well as you had hoped.

What exactly went wrong?

Go through 'REACH' again, and decide what to do next.

On the next page are the comments of two women managers on how they cope with their particular sources of stress.

Case studies

Catherine Carruthers, Project Manager, Business in the Community

> A number of things cause me stress in my job. One is feeling lack of control about the amount of work I have to do. Linked to that is the 7 days a week, 12 hours a day syndrome, because then I become tired and completely useless. I find that I need to be pushed to be effective . . . but not swamped.

> I have to eat and sleep well and also have some intellectual stimulation, which I get from music and the theatre. If I can do all these things in a week, then I can cope well with stress.

> Prioritising things helps tremendously. I find making a list of things to do and doing the worst one first is a good stress beater. My greatest enemy has always been perfectionism and the more I've learnt, the more I've recognised that things don't have to be perfect all of the time. I can now switch off and not worry about it. It's better if you can compromise some of the time.

Briony Jones, Project Manager, Automobile Association, Basingstoke

> Managing people who do not report directly to me, and having to achieve objectives which need their full support, can be very stressful — especially if any problems occur. Working for someone who sets tight deadlines would cause me stress, as I like to do a good job and may push myself unnecessarily hard to produce the goods in a shorter space of time.

> During the day, to relieve stress, I concentrate specifically on a problem in order to move it on a pace. I really feel I've achieved something then. I use a relaxation technique of self-hypnosis to break my day so I don't build and build on stress.

Do not expect to solve your problems overnight. Something which has caused you stress for a while will not necessarily disappear quickly. However, with determination and effort, you should find a way to relieve your stress — *your* way.

5
Tactics for Promotion

If you have overcome the blocks to success, defined your own management style, demonstrated your abilities on a regular basis in prominent activities, and feel you can cope with the pressures — you are in a good position to move for promotion.

This final chapter considers some strategies you can adopt to move up the career ladder, whether in your present organisation or outside it.

TEN TACTICS FOR PROMOTION

The main tactics for promotion are as follows:

1. Know yourself.
2. Set goals for yourself.
3. Improve yourself.
4. Use your initiative.
5. Be the best.
6. Let people know.
7. Be visible.
8. Find a mentor.
9. Assert yourself.
10. Believe in yourself.

Consider each of these in turn. You will find that most issues discussed in this chapter include an exercise for you to complete. These activities will help you to draw up your action plan at the end of the volume, which will become your own personal strategy for promotion. The first tactic is the most essential thing you must do to achieve promotion at any level.

Know yourself

You need to take charge of your own self-development in order to succeed in management. Gone are the days when employees could rely on their organisations to identify and develop 'high-flyers'. Even when management training schemes are available, the numbers of women who take advantage of them are still small.

If you want to be considered for the next promotion, you need to make sure you are prepared. Look at yourself objectively in order to identify your skills and qualities. Make a list of your possible weaknesses and analyse them. Do any of them present potential handicaps at the next level on the management ladder? When you have answered this question, you can decide whether you are prepared to change or will settle for less.

Identify your main management strengths and weaknesses. You will look at how to overcome the weaker areas in a moment.

Strengths	Weaknesses

Set goals for yourself

If you do not know where you are going, how will you know when you have arrived?

Goals are like dreams with deadlines. Setting long-term goals for yourself will require some in-depth thinking about your work, your personal life and your future. Ask yourself:

- 'What do I want to be doing in five years' time?'
- 'What do I need to do now to achieve this?'

You should be doing something each day to achieve your goal. Attaining your goal must be among your list of priorities. If it is not, you have little chance of achieving it. Once you have defined your goal, write it down, look at it regularly, and modify it if necessary.

If you know your goal, complete the chart below. If not, come back to it when you have thought it through in detail.

Goals

What do I want to be doing in five years' time?

```



```

What am I doing right now to achieve this?

If you feel you are not doing enough to achieve your goal, come back to this question when you have reviewed the other tactics for promotion.

Improve yourself

To recognise the areas where you need to improve, look at the skills needed at the next level and ask yourself what you are going to do to gain these skills. Look at people who have been promoted to similar jobs and assess what they can do that you cannot.

This should help you start a self-development programme of your own — and you must start it on your own. Nobody is going to offer you training on a plate, but if you need it, ask for it. Senior people have to see that you have all the necessary skills to operate at the next level before they can visualise you in that role.

If you know your goal, complete the activity on the next page.

Improving my prospects

What are my areas for improvement?

Where can I get the training or experience that I need?

What am I going to do about it?

When am I going to start?

If it is difficult to find out the information you need, speak to somebody who is in the job or in a position to appoint people to a similar job.

Use your initiative

If you want to advance, you have to use your initiative. Trust your own judgement and apply it to decisions which are within your area of control. Do not look to other people constantly for help and reassurance, or to make the decisions for you. Look for ways to demonstrate that you are competent and ambitious.

- Take on some of your manager's tasks.

Show that you are keen to improve your abilities and would regard any delegation from your manager as a new challenge. Tell your manager you would appreciate help in this area, in order that he or she does not feel threatened. In most cases it is important to *be seen* to back your boss, as he or she may be the first person to be consulted if you apply for promotion.

- Ask for extra responsibility.

If you feel you can handle a particular task you are not doing at the moment, put yourself forward for it. Do not forget that if you do this, you may have to shed some of your own responsibility to fulfil the new task effectively — you cannot do it all. If you try to do everything yourself, you could find that you do nothing well. You must be prepared to delegate.

- Volunteer for new projects.

If you are not considered for additional responsibility, ask yourself whether it is because people do not know that you want it. Demonstrate your motivation by stepping forward sometimes and showing that you are keen to 'have a go'.

- Look for gaps.

Take advantage of any opportunity to use and exploit your skills. These gaps may appear in your own or other departments. When people are ill or on holiday, look for ways of showing that you can handle certain aspects of their jobs too.

■ Take on tasks that others refuse.

If someone refuses to take on a task, decide if it might be advantageous to take it on yourself. Your boss may have a particular idea for improvement, but no time to work on the idea. That may be your chance.

■ Create some new ideas.

Look for new ways of tackling what may be routine tasks. Keep in mind that your solution should be practical and be seen as a high priority by management. When it succeeds, let others know about it and take the credit.

■ Take risks.

People do not grow if they do not take risks. For some women, the fear of failure is greater than the desire for success. To succeed, you have to put your initiative to the fore and not be frightened of what that might bring — whether it is success or failure.

In what ways can you demonstrate initiative at work? Select at least two tactics you could use; be specific.

Showing initiative

I can show initiative by:

Even if you are looking for promotion outside your present organisation, any tactic which will get you noticed should improve the quality of the reference that you get.

Be the best

You will not be noticed or singled out if you are average. Being the best involves commitment, energy and, above all, effort. Try to excel at what is important and leave the less important tasks to others. Being the best is vital for women because women often have to perform twice as well as men to be thought as good as men.

You do not just have to demonstrate your skills — you will have to do so with enthusiasm. People who are keen *and* enthusiastic are the ones who get noticed. A lethargic or even grudging approach does not win approval or promotion.

What can you do to demonstrate that you are the best at work?

How I can be the best

1.   What is your particular area of expertise?

<table><tr><td>

</td></tr></table>

2. Is there something in particular that only you can do? What is it?

3. What is the highest qualification in your field? Do you have it?

4. Do your knowledge and expertise relate to a major aspect of the organisation's work?

5. Do people frequently consult you and ask for your advice?

☐ YES   ☐ NO

6. If you were leaving your particular organisation, would management have difficulty in replacing you?

☐ YES   ☐ NO

7. Are you the best person at your particular job?

☐ YES   ☐ NO

If you answered 'yes' to Question 7, go to 8a; if you answered 'no', go to 8b.

8a. Are you recognised as the best?

☐ YES   ☐ NO

8b.   What tactics can you employ to be the best?

If you are the best at what you do and are recognised as such, you are definitely in a position to move ahead. If you are not the best, but want to be the best, look at your requirements, whether they be training, development or additional opportunities.

If you are the best at what you do, but are not recognised as such, you need to plan ways of demonstrating your skills. This might include taking on more high-profile tasks, writing more reports, highlighting your achievements, or simply telling your boss what a good job you are doing!

Let people know

Being good at your job does not guarantee you will be promoted. It does not even guarantee you will be noticed. You have to let people know you are ambitious and want to get ahead. Convince the powers that be that you have the qualities and skills necessary to achieve the promotion you want.

Equally, you want feedback on what you do. Ask your manager for a regular appraisal. Not only does such appraisal give you the opportunity to discuss areas for improvement, but it also emphasises your strengths to your manager.

Some male managers fear being totally honest with women staff lest they collapse emotionally if negative comments are made. You should actually welcome negatives. If you show that you can take criticism in a constructive manner, you can then take the necessary steps to improve.

Who are the people in power and what can you do to influence them? Answer the following questions.

How I will let people know

1.   Who are the people with the power to recommend promotion?

[   ]

2.   Do they know you are ambitious?

☐ YES   ☐ NO

If you answered 'yes' to Question 2, go to 3a; if you answered 'no', go to 3b.

3a. Is there anything you can do, which you are not already doing, to convince them?

3b. What strategies could you employ to demonstrate your ambition?

The vigour with which you promote yourself within the organisation is even more crucial to your success if you work in an organisation which is reluctant or unaccustomed to promote women in management.

Be visible

Get to know the people who count and let them know who you are, what you are doing, and where you want to go. Becoming visible is an essential part of getting the credit due to you and increasing your number of career options.

To get yourself into the limelight, there are a number of things you can do. Some have already been discussed. Others include:

- altering your personal style and image;
- organising social events;
- speaking up at meetings;
- chairing meetings;
- telling people your name and function if meeting them for the first time — whether inside or outside the organisation;
- getting credit for things you have done well;
- finding out the best place to be seen and getting yourself there.

How can you increase your visibility at work? Make some suggestions relevant to your present, or intended, place of work.

Being seen

Increasing my visibility:

Find a mentor

A mentor can help, support and advise you in your quest for promotion. This may be your present manager, a more senior manager (if organisational politics allow), or a colleague at a similar level but with more experience. It does not matter who acts as your mentor, male or female, as long as you have a relationship based on mutual respect and trust.

The value of a mentor is often misunderstood. Having a mentor does not mean 'trying to get in through the back door', and your mentor is not your role model. A mentor is a person with more experience than you who will give valuable feedback on your ideas, and advice on career progression. A mentor is also a tremendous asset as a supporter — for the times when you doubt your own abilities and feel less than confident; someone to say, 'Yes, you can do it.'

Is there anyone who could act as your mentor? If there is more than one possibility, write them all below.

Who could be my mentor?

1.

2.

3.

If you have not identified anyone, there is an alternative approach. You could join one of the many networks for women which now flourish in various parts of the country. Networks provide a forum for socialising and making good business contacts. They usually organise lectures, seminars and training events, which could provide you with the advice and information you need.

Assert yourself

Self-confidence and a positive approach lay the foundations for a successful management career. Do not let people manipulate you into doing what they want or what they think you should do. You need to be strong and to be seen to be strong. Confidence and competence are natural allies. Make sure they are both on your side!

Believe in yourself

Make your own success; do not wait for it to be handed to you on a plate. People who are successful often credit it to good luck, when luck has very little to do with it. What you believe about yourself helps to determine what actually happens. In everything that you do, try to establish the personal attitude that you can handle anything. If you do not have the knowledge, skills or information now, you have the personal resources to acquire them. Remember, the woman who wins is the one who thinks she can!

Here are some comments from other senior-status women on their tactics for promotion.

- 'Don't imitate others — operate from your own female strengths.'
- 'Know yourself and what type of work makes you happy.'
- 'Get all the training you need for your *next* job — if it's not forthcoming, ask or even demand.'
- 'If you take a career break, stay in touch. But don't apologise for having children.'
- 'Don't pitch your expectations too low — this tends to rub off on other people.'
- 'Get a mentor so that you can draw on the experience of someone in a more senior position.'

■ 'Don't feel defeated; never give up — and you'll manage to succeed.'

The following case studies show the views of two women managers.

Case studies

Anna Gilbert, Airport Duty Manager, Manchester Airport

It's important to look for opportunities and go for them, while at the same time enjoying the job and knowing you will be capable of performing well. Men have networks, both formal and informal, to help them when they're planning for promotion. I believe women need to become part of such networks, or build their own, in order to improve their circle of contacts.

Christine Lyles, Equal Opportunities Manager, Barclays Bank, London

A course I attended some time ago for women managers made me focus on what I wanted to achieve in the long term, in a way I had never done before. I had never really set myself goals, and the course led to me make a conscious decision to do this. Previously, I was almost apologising for having worked in Personnel for ten years. Now I'm turning this to my advantage, and my first step has been to gain management entry into the IPM.

Action Plan

Now it is time to draw up your personal action plan; that is, things you are going to start doing, or stop doing, in your own preparations for promotion.

To help you formulate your plan, you may like to refer to certain chapters of this volume and some of the exercises you completed. You may like to look at:

- overcoming blocks to success;
- improving leadership potential;
- female strengths;
- improving presentation skills;
- how to be more effective in meetings;
- the REACH Strategy for coping with stress;
- ten tactics for promotion.

Here is an extract from one woman's action plan:

Things I am going to start/stop doing	*Made a start*	*Getting there*	*Doing well*
1. Stop feeling devastated when I make a mistake.	✔ 5 Aug		
2. Formulate my career goal	✔ 7 Aug	✔ 20 Aug	
3. Attend training course on time management	✔ 9 Sept (applied)		Done!

This is how to write your own action plan.

How to write an action plan — step by step

1. Select *three* things you are going to start/stop doing in your personal preparations for promotion. Start with something relatively easy, in order to see the results quickly.

2. Write them down in the left-hand column.

3. Come back to the list in a week and review your progress.

4. When you have achieved what you resolved to do, tick the column and date it.

5. When you have achieved your goal on three occasions or have completed the task you set yourself, you are entitled to feel pleased with your progress. You have achieved what you set out to do.

6. As you complete one task, add others to the bottom of the list. An action plan is an ongoing process.

Things I am going to start/stop doing	Made a start	Getting there	Doing well

Things I am going to start/stop doing	Made a start	Getting there	Doing well

The secret is not to work on too many tasks at one time. Take things a step at a time and progress to more difficult areas later rather than sooner.

If you find that the changes you make are effective, they will probably become routine within a short time. If you find that something does not work immediately, do not give up too soon; persevere, as certain changes take time. Habits of a lifetime cannot be changed overnight, particularly if they affect the life and work of others.

If certain things do not seem to be working, look for other techniques that work for you. Come back to your action plan from time to time and make the changes which will suit you.

If things are working, yet promotion does not seem to be on offer, perhaps it is time to formulate your biggest action plan. Look for another organisation which will appreciate your skills, talents and senior management abilities.

Good luck in your preparations for promotion!

Further Reading

Alkenson, Jacqueline (1988) *Coping with Stress at Work*, Thorsons, Wellingborough.

Armstrong, Michael (1990) *How to be an Even Better Manager*, Kogan Page, London.

Bryce, Lee (1989) *The Influential Woman*, Piatkus, London.

Chambers, C, Cooper, S and McLean, A (1990) *Develop Your Management Potential*, Kogan Page, London.

Chapman, Elwood (1988) *How to Develop a Positive Attitude*, Kogan Page, London.

Cooper, Cary and Davidson, Marilyn (1984) *Women In Management*, Heinemann, London.

—— and Lewis, S (1989) *Career Couples*, Unwin, London.

Courtis, John (1988) *44 Most Common Management Mistakes*, Kogan Page, London.

Crabtree, Stan (1981) *Moving Up*, Kogan Page, London.

Davidson, Marilyn (1985) *Reach For The Top*, Piatkus, London.

Dickson, Ann (1985) *A Woman In Your Own Right*, Quartet, London.

Dyer, Wayne (1985) *Pulling Your Own Strings* Hamlyn, Twickenham.

—— (1986) *Your Erroneous Zone*, Sphere, London.

Ernst & Young (1991) *The Manager's Self-Assessment Kit*, Kogan Page, London.

Evans, R and Russell, P (1989) *The Creative Manager*, Unwin, London.

Further Information

Business in the Community
227A City Road
London EC1
Tel: 071-253 3716

Confederation of British
Industry
Centre Point
103 New Oxford Street
London WC1A 1DU
Tel: 071-379 7400

Domino Consultancy Ltd
56 Charnwood Road
Shepshed
Leicestershire LE12 9NP
Tel: 0509 505404

Equal Opportunities
Commission
Overseas House
Quay Street
Manchester M3 3HN
Tel: 061-833 9244

European Women's
Management Development
Network
EWMD Secretariat
c/o EFMD
40 Rue Washington
Brussels
Belgium
UK Secretary: Christine Barham
Tel: 0442 843491

Industrial Society: Pepperell
Unit
Robert Hyde House
48 Bryanston Square
London W1H 7LN
Tel: 071-262 2401

Trade Union Congress
Great Russell Street
London WC1
Tel: 071-636 4030

United Kingdom Federation of
Business and Professional
Women
23 Ansdell Street
London W8 5BN
Tel: 071-938 1729

Women in Management
64 Marryat Road
Wimbledon
London SW19 5BN
Tel: 081-944 6332

Fisher, Roger and Ury, William (1986) *Getting to Yes*, Hutchinson, London.

Haddock, Patricia and Manning, Marylyn (1989) *Leadership Skills for Women*, Kogan Page, London.

Hansard Society Commission (1990) *Women at the Top*, Hansard Society, London.

Haynes, Marion (1988) *Effective Meeting Skills*, Kogan Page, London.

Lindley, Patricia and Makin, Peter (1991) *Positive Stress Management*, Kogan Page, London.

Lloyd, Sam (1988) *How to Develop Assertiveness*, Kogan Page, London.

McDonald, Janet (1986) *Climbing the Ladder*, Methuen, London.

Minzberg, Henry (1973) *The Nature of Managerial Work*, Harper and Row, New York.

Moates-Kennedy, Marilyn (1984) *Powerbase: How to Built It, How to Keep It*, Fawcett Crest, Wetherby.

Morris, M J (1988) *First Time Manager*, Kogan Page, London.

National Economic Development Office (NEDO) (1990) *Women Managers*, Kogan Page, London.

Paul, Nancy (1984) *The Right to be You*, Chartwell Bratt, Bromley.

Powell, G N (1988) *Women and Men in Management*, Sage, London.

Rhodes, J and Thame, S (1988) *The Colours of Your Mind*, Fontana, London.

Shaevitz, Marjorie (1984) *The Superwoman Syndrome*, Fontana, London.

Siewart, Lothar (1989) *Managing Your Time*, Kogan Page, London.

Skinner, Jane and Fritchie, Rennie (1988) *Working Choices*, J M Dent, London.

Spenser, L and Young, K (1990) *Women Managers in Local Government: Removing the Barriers*, LGMB, London.

Women Returners' Network (1991) *Returning to Work*, Kogan Page, London.